Anna Vivanti

A Journey to Crete, Constantinople, Naples, and Florence

Three months abroad

Anna Vivanti

A Journey to Crete, Constantinople, Naples, and Florence
Three months abroad

ISBN/EAN: 9783744755696

Printed in Europe, USA, Canada, Australia, Japan

Cover: Foto ©Andreas Hilbeck / pixelio.de

More available books at **www.hansebooks.com**

A JOURNEY

TO

CRETE, CONSTANTINOPLE, NAPLES, AND FLORENCE.

THREE MONTHS ABROAD.

BY

ANNA VIVANTI.

LONDON:
PRINTED FOR PRIVATE CIRCULATION.
1865.

Dedication.

TO MY HUSBAND.

To Thee, whose hand has kindly led me forth
   Far o'er the land, across the deep blue sea,
Whose care and love watch'd o'er me every where,
   I dedicate this little History.

May it recall to thee the motley crowd
   Of strange and kindly people we have seen,
The golden days of the enchanted Isle,
   How wondrous bright and happy they have been.

The smiling Bosphorus and grand Stamboul,
   The glorious bay of beauteous Napoli,
The festive days at Florence,—and accept
   This as a sign of gratitude from me.

    LOWER NORWOOD,
       Dec. 1st, 1865.

CONTENTS.

CHAPTER I.

	PAGE
FROM LONDON TO CRETE	1

CHAPTER II.

CRETE, OR THE ENCHANTED ISLAND	40

CHAPTER III.

CONSTANTINOPLE	90

CHAPTER IV.

FROM CONSTANTINOPLE TO FLORENCE	126

CHAPTER V.

THE DANTE FESTIVAL AT FLORENCE	157

THREE MONTHS ABROAD.

CHAPTER I.

FROM LONDON TO CRETE.

"O Wandern, Wandern, meine Lust! O Wandern."
W. Müller.

It was on the morning of the 18th of March, 1865, that, "equipped from top to toe," I kissed all my little ones, shook hands with the kind friends who were to take care of them, and started with my husband on our grand wedding tour. Yes, this was to be our wedding tour; for the one we made directly after our wedding, more than ten years ago, did not deserve that name; and since then we had never travelled without, what is most properly called encumbrances, not meaning trunks or bandboxes, but babies of different sizes and ages. Our first wedding trip! Shall I confess that it did not extend farther than Broadstairs! How times change! Our wishes were more limited then; I am sure we thought we had gone quite as far as people could wish to go, for we went by water, and the weather being rather windy, we were both very nearly sea-sick when we arrived. But no more of these old bye-gone times, I have other things to tell. When we drove off, and I looked once more back, my baby clapped her little fat hands together, and called out, " Lumps of delight, lumps of delight." A turban! a sword! a drum! screamed the boys, and off we drove on our way to Crete. Yes, to Crete! where nobody has ever been that I know of, since Theseus.

But before we got there, we arrived at London Bridge. There we met dear Mme. M———, whom we had promised to see safely to Cologne. She is the mother of one of the greatest scholars of our time, and the widow of one who would certainly have been one of the greatest German poets, had he not died at the age of thirty-three.

On the evening of the 18th we arrived safely and well at Brussels, and had a few hours time before the train started for Cologne. So we set out for a short stroll through the town by gas-light. It looked just as I had thought it would look, gay and lively. " A little Paris," as it is so often called. The " Galleries" reminded me of the Palais Royal, and the people that leisurely walked about seemed as well dressed, and as much " on pleasure bent," as those of the Boulevards.

The shops where "knicknacks" are sold look as elegant as those of Paris, and in others there is the same delightful display of fruit and flowers, delicacies, and confectionary.

I could, of course, not walk through the streets and market-place of Brussels without thinking of Egmont and Hoorn, and of the splendid scene in Goethe's Egmont, where Klärchen calls upon the people to save her lover. I also remembered the poor sisters, Charlotte and Emily Brontë. My husband thought of Napoleon and Wellington, and Becky Sharp, and laughed again at the thought of Jos Sedley's flight from Brussels.

With an appetite stimulated by the walk, the keen March air, and the very inviting exhibition of dainties in several shop-windows, we dined, and then left for Cologne, where we arrived at five in the morning, and parted from Mme. M——, our dear friend, for such she had become to us, we feeling rather anxious how she would get on without us; she full of gratitude for the little we had been able to do for her, blessing us many times, and wishing us a safe return to our children; to which I said "Amen," with all my heart.

As we had a few hours to spare before the train started for Coblentz, we went out to look at the Cathedral, which I had not seen for several years. I was pleased to see that the giant work has advanced much in that comparatively short time; they told me it would be quite finished in about six years, but that I humbly doubt.

It was a wretchedly cold morning; a sharp easterly wind blowing, which after a night passed in a railway carriage, seemed to freeze me. It chilled my love for the beautiful. I was not very deeply impressed; not even by the interior of the Cathedral, although I know it is wondrous grand and beautiful.

What a comfortable hotel, "The Giant," at Coblentz is! And how we enjoyed our dinner at the table d'hôte, sitting down to it like civilized people after a thorough toilette. As March is not the time for English tourists on the Rhine, we had, instead of whispered English conversation, the loud talk of the Prussian officers, who had the table almost to themselves. They were most of them fine looking men, and had such a number of stars and crosses, and medals, that after seeing them I wondered that there should be still some poor little Danes left alive. I thought that these young giants must have killed them all, being all so distinguished for valour, which many of them were too young to have proved even against the rebels in Baden in 1848.

After dinner we drove to Stolzenfels, and enjoyed the view, which all who have seen it will remember with pleasure. I had looked from Stolzenfels upon Lahneck and Upper and Lower Lahnstein, when the hills that rise behind were covered with the glory of September foliage; but even without that gay dress, the scene is lovely still. We drove back to the hotel in spirits that were in harmony with the bright scene around us and the merry people that animated it. The influence of the fine continental air and the bright sunshine upon the spirits of those who have breathed the thick air of London for a whole year, with the exception perhaps of a few months at Brighton, is wonderfully exhilarating. All who have experienced it must wish for the Continent again and again, and will prefer to spend the autumn abroad, although the English lakes, Wales and Scotland, offer perhaps as much scenic beauty as Germany or France.

On the morning of the 20th we left Coblentz, and went by rail to Mayence, passing the most beautiful spots of the Rhine, enjoying it much, and forming the resolution to buy one of the ruined castles, restore it and live for ever on the Rhine, with a boat to row on the river and a guitar to accompany the German ballads we would sing on a summer evening. At Mayence we left the Rhine, and turned eastward across the Hessian plains towards Bavaria. The cold wind we had now to face made us shut all the windows, and I must confess in spite of my belonging to the Ladies' Sanitary Association, and having read Florence Nightingale's book and Combe's too, we shut also the ventilators, and unstrapped all our shawls and wrappers. I looked wistfully at the snow that had appeared on the ground soon after we left Mayence, and which grew thicker and thicker, glittering in the sunshine, like a cold beauty that smiles but does not melt. The sky was perfectly cloudless, the sun brilliant and warm, the wind cutting and sharp; the shades deep and cold; after sunset the window panes became covered with frost, but not like in England, where it springs up in a very short time, and afterwards disappears as quickly, and which is of a poor tame pattern, always resembling artichoke leaves. Here the cold worked slowly, deliberately and elaborately, like a careful artist: each pane became a picture, showing a variety of beautiful and fanciful shapes and forms, flowers, miniature forests, multitudes of stars, brilliants and crystals. Gradually, it shut us completely out from the world, and after we had passed Nuremberg and Erlangen, we heard and saw no more of it, till we arrived at Passau, the Austrian frontier, where people have to undergo the ordeal of the douane.

We arrived there at 2 o'clock in the morning and had to extricate ourselves from shawls and wrappers in order to be present at the examination of our luggage. On re-entering the carriage, the guard told us that there were sixteen degrees of frost,* after which information, I felt that I had a right to shiver and to complain. The guard himself wrapped up in an immense fur, wearing top-boots lined with fur, and a fur cap drawn over his ears, looked provokingly cheerful and comfortable, and told me when he heard my grumbling at the cold, that in spite of that it was much better there than in England where, that he knew for certain, the sun, even in the month of June, was never visible before 9 o'clock in the morning, for till then there was always fog and mist. He had been in London, but did not like it at all. The coffee was horrible, although he suspected with much acuteness, that it was partly the fault of the milk. The tea was worse still, for they gave no rum with it, and tea without rum was little better than hot water, and he concluded, "how can you expect an Austrian to live in a place where six

---

* 16° Reaumur equal to 36° of Fahrenheit.

cigars cost a shilling or more? What are six cigars a day for a man that likes them?" There were but two things in London that had pleased him, the Crystal Palace and Mme. Tussaud's Exhibition. The wax figures of that celebrated artist had made a deep impression upon him. We found in Vienna the weather as cold and ungenial as on our journey; but feeling that it would have been a shame not to see something of the town, we walked and drove about, and were glad when we had performed that troublesome duty.

Schönbrunnen alone, which awakens so many recollections, aroused also some degree of interest in me. The pretty pictures painted by the Emperor Francis I., especially those he painted on the fans of his wife Maria Theresa, the embroidery of that great woman, the drawings of her unhappy and beautiful daughter, Maria Antoinette, the family portraits of the Hapsburghs, down to the present Empress and her sisters, the room in which the Duc de Reichstadt died, his portrait as a fair and beautiful boy; all that interested me much. The gardens and park surrounding this pretty summer residence were still covered with snow, and the air was so cold that I was glad to get back again to the hotel, where, looking in Continental fashion from the window into the street, I spent some pleasant hours. The passers by although less elegant in appearance than in Paris, look more picturesque and appear in a much greater variety of costume. All the ladies wear large fur capes and large muffs. Many have also their little hats and bonnets trimmed with fur, and the young girls tripping along briskly, look decidedly pretty. I liked also the costume of the Hungarian men. They wear top-boots, short braided coats lined and trimmed with fur, and high fur caps. Many of the peasants of the different provinces of Austria have also a very picturesque appearance.

If the days, on account of the weather, were not the most enjoyable, the evenings were all the more so. We spent them in the theatre. Now the Burg Theatre of Vienna is old, ugly, and dark; but perfectly comfortable, and the acting first-rate; and to see first-rate acting is a great enjoyment. All the Viennese seem to think so too, for the Theatre was filled in every part; and one evening the Imperial box was adorned by the presence of the beautiful Empress of Austria. Everybody who has visited the Exhibition of 1862, and who has not been there? must recollect the charming portrait of the Empress. She is quite as beautiful, indeed even more so, for the portrait showed only the face, not her elegant commanding figure, and graceful movements. There were beside her in the box, the father of the Emperor, the Archduchess Sophia, and Count Trani, brother of the ex-King of Naples.

The journey from Vienna to Trieste must in summer be very beautiful, but when we took it, although it was already the 23rd of March, there were 10 degrees of cold,* enough to chill anybody that is neither a Russian nor Polar Bear. My husband was much interested, and declared the railroad across the Alps one of the finest works of modern engineering. The railway winds ziz-zag up the mountain like the road over the Splugen, or the Mont Cenis. But the wind was cutting and cold; the snow that fell incessantly penetrated even through the closed windows. We had left Vienna in the morning; about six o'clock at night we arrived at Semmering, which is the highest point. Here the snow lay mountain deep. I had never seen it in such masses. What a feeling of solitude and desolation, deep, far-extending snow gives one. It covers the earth like a shroud. The sea in winter with a leaden sky, is a lively cheerful thing, compared to such a snowy desert. I saw in the waning light, a man at some distance,

* 22½ F.

plodding apparently with difficulty through it. How lost and desolate he seemed. I was quite glad when I discovered about two miles farther on a house, from the chimney of which a thin column of smoke arose, and which I thought was probably the end of his journey; where at all events he would find shelter. Beyond Semmering, the road for many miles leads along the top of deep precipices, to look down which while travelling in a train gives one anything but a feeling of security. Wherever the road is not protected from the North wind by the mountains, there are strong high oaken palings to shelter it, for the Bora, a north-easterly gale, blows here often with such violence, that unless protected by the mountain or these palings, the whole train might be easily overthrown and hurled down some precipice. Near Adelsberg, where we arrived about midnight, the train came suddenly to a standstill; the snow being so deep on the line, that the engine could not move on. Like a good horse, it seemed to try its utmost to pull us through, but all its efforts resulted in some very uncomfortable shakings it gave us while endeavouring to push through the snow.

After about an hour's delay they had cleared the line sufficiently for the train to move on, and in the morning we arrived at Trieste. It is a pretty modern town, in a charming situation. The villas which are scattered over the hills, that rise behind the town, look very pretty and pleasant. "Mira Mare," the property of Prince Maximilian of Austria, Emperor of Mexico, is a beautiful marine residence. The streets of Trieste are paved as those of Florence, Naples, and Messina, with large stones, like our London footpaths, they present an animated appearance, for one sees many different costumes. I remember, especially that of the Mexican soldiers, of which there were many in Trieste, and who, in their long white woollen cloaks, and broad-brimmed straw hats, are wild and picturesque-looking fellows.

All the day there blew a strong north-easterly wind, which the Triestines however, called a Boretta, meaning a little Bora; but I must confess that in spite of that, I looked rather suspiciously at the many little white-headed waves of the Adriatic, which looked just the kind to give one an incipient sea-sickness; considering that we were to embark the next afternoon for a five days' sea voyage, and that possibly the Boretta might become a Bora. This time however, I was luckier than I had hoped. The sun rose the next day in a cloudless sky, and when I looked out of my window, the flags on the masts of the ships, lying in the harbour, waved gently, instead of violently turning and twisting about as they had done the day before; and the sea was smooth and smiling as "The Bride of the Doges" at Venice, which I had seen, and remembered with delight.

In high spirits therefore, we went on board the Lloyd steamer "Neptune," which was to take us to Sira, I had but one bad foreboding. We had been told, that as it was so early in the year, we might chance to have the boat almost entirely to ourselves. As I am of a sociable disposition, I did not relish the idea of being locked up in a large ship without travelling companions.

How agreeably surprised was I therefore, to find the deck absolutely crowded when we arrived, and not by chance travellers, but by forty excursionists to the Holy Land, who wished to spend the Easter week at Jerusalem. I at once anticipated an interesting and singular company, very different from every-day tourists, and I was not mistaken. I became more or less acquainted with many of them, and they made the five days of our voyage together pass very pleasantly. The great majority of them were Germans from all parts of the Fatherland; but there were also a few Hungarians and Poles, four Americans, and one old Italian amongst them. They all belonged to the "lords of creation," with the exception of two who were of the gentle sex, that wears crinoline. This mixed company I divided, however, into two classes only; the devout and the profane, viz. those that went, or said they went, to the Holy Land from devotion, and those that avowed they were going there from different motives.

Of those belonging to the first class, the old Polish General, Count T——, in consideration of his high position and great age, deserves to be mentioned first. He was an old man of 77, with an enormous appetite, who said that he had not tasted water he could remember when, and believed he would be ill if he ventured to drink any. He had spent his life on horseback, and looked as hale and strong as a young man. His head was of a very peculiar shape. A phrenologist would have said that in it the propensities preponderated largely over the sentiments. His white hair and long white moustache could not make him look venerable. I was glad when he told me that he was going to Jerusalem for devotion, for I felt sure he had plenty of cause for repentance, he looked such a sensual old sinner.

In his manners he was pleasant and gallant, and his conversation was not uninteresting. He had travelled much, been every where; and seemed especially to remember all the places famous for beautiful women. There were two Catholic priests among the passengers. One a Curé from Galicia, a young man, with a thin bent figure, a sickly voice, and spare fair hair; looking altogether more an object of pity than of interest; the other a young, yet venerable looking Dominican friar, with a beautiful face and fine oriental beard. I was sorry that I understood neither Polish nor Latin, the only languages he spoke; for I think he had many interesting things to tell. His convent in Warsaw had been lately abolished by the Russian Government, and the poor friars who were suspected of having Polish sympathies were now wandering beggars, so the Curé told me. This one was, however, a very comfortable and venerable looking beggar, and seemed to be well provided with more than friars are supposed to require, viz. warm stockings and strong shoes and a large wide-a-wake hat. An old Italian sailor, owner of some barges, which were now managed by his sons, was going to the Holy Land, from a beautiful sentiment of pure devotion and gratitude. He had been prosperous in his trade and fortunate in his family. All his sons were doing well, all his daughters happily married. He had lost his wife many years ago, but time and religion had soothed that sorrow. He was going to Jerusalem now to offer there thanks to the Divine Being for the joys of a long and honourable existence, to pray for the soul of his departed wife, and for the salvation of all his children. He showed me a letter from his youngest daughter, in whose house the old man lived, and who had sent him this letter to Trieste. It was badly spelt, but most touching. She called upon the Holy Virgin and all the saints to take her dear father under their kind and powerful protection and bring him safely back to his home, which seemed desolate without him. The old sailor was of great use to me, he knew, as he called it, ' every stone of the coast,' and was always willing and often able to tell me what I wanted to know about the places we passed. When we arrived at Corfù, he went on shore, but not from any curiosity, the place was well known to him, but in order to perform his devotions at the silver shrine of St. Spiridion, the patron saint of the island. At Sira, where there seemed to be no particular saint, he did not leave the boat; it is a new town, and in our times saints seem to have become scarce. But if the old sailor seemed to be intent upon nothing but praying to all the saints on the road, a little German master miller had apparently undertaken this pilgrimage in order only to buy photographs of all sizes and descriptions at every place we stopped at. Not knowing any other language but Viennese-German, he must have had sometimes great difficulty in accomplishing his object in places where people understood only Greek and Italian. But where there is a will there is a way. He seemed to find by instinct the places where photographs were to be got, and succeeded in buying some very nice ones in Corfù, where I, not being equally persevering, had failed in procuring any. When we arrived in Sira, the funny little man, as soon as he reached the land by means of a boat that had taken several of his companions ashore, left them who were satisfied with seeing in reality what he wanted on cardboard. While they were going up the hill, on which the Roman Catholic church stands, and from whence there is a fine view over the town, the harbour, and the sea, he remained in the town in search of photographs. This time, however, he was destined to be disappointed; for, although he found a place where they sold photographs, and where they showed him many, he found they were views of every place and country in the world, especially of Paris and Vienna; but not of so common a place as Sira, which every one there had always before his eyes. In looking over all the photographs in search of those he wished, the time must have passed more rapidly than he was aware of, for he was not at the " embarcader" when his travelling companions arrived there, in order to return to the boat. The wind that was fresh when they landed had much increased, and the boatmen told them they had better get on board the steamer as soon as possible, and after waiting a little while, they did as they were advised, and left the poor little miller behind. When he arrived at the place of embarcation, the Greeks somehow made him understand that the others had left Sira, and that he must take a boat for himself. By this time the wind had become very strong, and when we perceived the boat that carried the little miller, the waves were constantly breaking over it, wetting him to the skin, and what was worst of all, spoiling his new beaver hat, which he had put on to go to Sira in, for what reason is best known to himself. When the two boatmen at last boarded the vessel, the rapacious Greeks asked so exorbitant a price for their trouble that the little German, although in great fear and longing to get on board, would not pay it, when they pushed off from the steamer again, one thrusting his hand in the terrified traveller's pocket with the intention of paying himself. At that moment one of the officers of the steamer observed the danger he was in, and came to his rescue by telling the Greeks in an imperious voice to put the poor man immediately on board.

The four young Americans that belonged to the party went to the Holy Land for the same purpose as they had visited England, France and Germany, viz. to see what the place was like. They were four modest and courteous young gentlemen; and if their Christian names had not been Lucius and Homer, and such like, and if they had not called the Russians " Rooshions" and America " Merico," I should not have " guessed" where they came from. Homer was evidently smitten with Mdlle. S——, one of the lady travellers; and always on the watch for an opportunity of offering her his opera glass or fetch a chair for her. The worldliest of the worldly was Mr. St——, a painter from Düsseldorf, a young man with a satirical face and roguish disposition. He was as good a sailor as the Captain, and enjoyed his meals as if he worked with a spade instead of a brush and pencil. He tried to flirt with the ladies, and drew most charming sketches of land and people. The portraits of General T—— and the little Jew doctor of the ship, were wonderfully true and humorous. He was always either drawing or talking, and delighted in teasing the poor curé, who generally answered in a gentle and becoming manner.

Between the devotees and the worldlings, belonging to both and yet to neither, uniting in himself all their good qualities and apparently free from their faults, stood Mr. H————, a clergyman from Cologne. A man of most venerable looks, highly cultivated mind, and a warm pious heart. With him I spent some of the pleasantest hours of our journey to Smyrna. He told me that for thirty years a journey to the Holy Land had been his wish by day, and his dream by night. When at last it was to be realised, his wife from mistaken kindness had much opposed it; had used entreaties and tears to prevent what she considered a dangerous journey; but the wish had been all too strong, she had been obliged to let him go. His face had a bright look of happiness, softened by what seemed a stronger and deeper feeling still—gratitude. And that bright look did not vanish, even when between Corfu and Sira, the sea became very rough, and prostrated most of the company, that had been so lively till then. When I asked him how he was, he answered with a smile, "To be or not to be, that is the question"! When, as we neared Sira, the sea became calmer, and that troublesome question was satisfactorily settled, I enjoyed his conversation again. When he spoke, the land and islands we passed, became peopled with gods and heroes. He did not, like M. R——, from Paris, who came on board our boat at Sira, chill my heart by telling me that there never was a Homer; that at the time when the songs of the Iliad and Odyssey originated, hundreds could sing in that style, as in the 17th century almost everybody in France could write a good letter, while in the 18th, nobody could.

Mr. H—— was no sceptic, and when I declared myself in favour of Chio, as the birth-place of the great bard, he said it was not impossible that I was right.

But I shall never get to Smyrna, if I describe all my travelling companions on the way, so I must come to an end, not however before I have said a few words of the two ladies. Mme. de H——, a Hungarian lady, sister of the Archbishop of Carthage, and formerly a governess to some of the grand-children of Louis Philippe, was a strong minded woman. She had been a widow these twenty years, but not having been very happy in her first union, had never yielded again to a proposal of marriage, although many had been made to her since. She said she was very much shocked and grieved, that so many of her companions should go to the Holy Land from curiosity, or seeking amusement; but I must confess that for a pilgrim to the Holy Land, she was rather gaily dressed. The cap she used to wear in the morning, when she appeared " en negligée," especially surprised me, being trimmed with (what my boys would have called) stunning bright green ribbon.

She had travelled much, and seen a good deal of the world and its life. She spoke indifferent French with a loud voice, and had generally two veils over her face to protect her complexion, trying to remedy defective sight by looking at one through an eye-glass.

Fräulein S—— was a pretty girl of eighteen, who went to Jerusalem "because Papa took her there," and he went there, as he had gone to many other places, for the simple love of change and travelling. She was, as I said, pretty, wore a neat becoming travelling dress, and was of course the centre of attraction to all the young men of the party. But being engaged to be married (this she told me in private), and apparently of a naturally modest and retiring disposition, the young men found it difficult to approach her. She stayed a great deal in the ladies' saloon, writing long letters, which I suppose went to Prague, where she was shortly going to live.

After a pleasant voyage of about forty-eight hours, we arrived at the island of Corfu, which is separated from the mainland by a small sheet of water only, resembling a lake rather than the sea; for when one nears the town of Corfu, the water seems entirely enclosed by land, and the view is then most charming. On the left, the rocky coast of Albania looks wild and picturesque; while the island to your right, covered by a luxuriant vegetation, has altogether a smiling and cheerful aspect.

But how strange and new everything appeared to me when we arrived at Corfu, the country, the town, the people. Fifty hours before I had been among mountains of snow, in an almost Siberian cold. Here, under a golden sun, palm trees were growing, and roses and geraniums were in full bloom. When we had gone on shore, we went through dirty, narrow little streets, up to the Spianata, a beautiful promenade, where the palace stands in which the English Lord High Commissioner formerly resided. I was sorry to think that this beautiful land enjoys no longer the blessing of English protection, under which it would surely have prospered. It has not much chance of doing so now.

Mr. H——, from Cologne, reminded me that Corfu was old Scheria, where King Alkinous lived, whose beautiful, innocent daughter, Nausikaa, the "lily-armed maiden," had saved the life of the noble sufferer Ulysses.

Before we had gone on shore, about a hundred Montenegrian labourers, going to Constantinople, came on board our vessel; their arrival, in about ten boats, was the strangest thing I had ever witnessed; the noise, the violent gesticulations, the scramble in getting on board, was indescribable, and quite frightened and perplexed me, who had not yet become accustomed to such manners. Some, finding that they could not approach the steps that led up to the deck, climbed like cats up the side of the vessel; and their luggage, consisting of dirty bundles, was hurled after them by their companions below. They wore the Greek costume, which is becoming and picturesque, loose blue pantaloons instead of trousers; a white, or coloured shirt, and a red fez for a head covering. Feet and legs were bare, and over their shoulders hung a shaggy cloak, with a three-cornered capuch to it. Their features were generally good; the straight line of the Greek profile well defined in many. They had lively eyes, and a profusion of dark curly hair.

When, after a few hours stroll through the town, and on the Spianata, we returned to the boat, I found that we had also an addition to our saloon passengers. They were all Greeks. One of them was M. Brilas, who had just been called to Athens to fill the office of Foreign Minister there. His only child, a fine, intelligent looking boy, accompanied him. A fortnight after, at the festivities in commemoration of the Greek Revolution, the boy had a sunstroke, and died. I grieved for the poor father when I heard of it. Mr. Conemenos, with his wife, also embarked at Corfu. He is a Greek, in the diplomatic service of the Ottoman Empire. Between myself and his young wife, an amiable and accomplished lady, an almost friendly relation soon sprang up. I was sorry to part from her at Sira, and promised to go and see her when I got to Constantinople, to which place she was now going on a visit to her parents. And there came another young Greek on board, whom I remember only because he was very beautiful, and looked exactly as

Homer describes some of the "curly-headed Achaians." He sat at meal-times next to General T——, and nearly opposite me. The contrast they formed was most striking. It being Lent, the pale-faced young Greek ate nothing but a little bread, and a few olives, while the old soldier, with his florid complexion, swallowed at breakfast alone, four eggs, a quantity of garlick sausage, and uncooked ham, besides fish and fowl, potatoes and rice.

The weather, which had been so fine on our way to Corfu, did not continue so favourable. The Sirocco blew fresh against us, and gradually the sea became very rough. The vessel rocked so much, that I did not care to remain long on deck, but retired early to my little cabin. I am a good sailor, and therefore did not suffer, but I slept little that night, being disturbed by the movements of the ship, which near Cape Matapan became lively in the extreme. How disappointing it is in such a night to wake after a short doze, thinking it must be near morning, and to find that it is just eleven o'clock, then dozing again, waking up with a start, and discovering by the dim light of the cabin lamp that it is not yet one. And how glad one feels when the morning dawns through the thick little pane of glass, and the scrubbing of the deck is heard overhead. Now it is day; the terrors of the night are passed, fear vanishes like an uneasy dream. And how refreshing is the morning breeze on the still wet deck, when the foaming sea begins to look blue and clear again, and the sun breaks forth through the clouds. The Montenegrians on the foredeck, also seemed to enjoy the bright morning after the rough night they had spent there. They made an early breakfast of brown bread, curd-cheese, and garlick; and looked very happy in their picturesque rags. A lad who sat on a kind of mat, his legs crossed, smoking a long Turkish pipe, looked the image of contemplative contentment. After another rough night we arrived the next morning in Sira, from whence we intended to proceed to Crete. Unfortunately there was no boat leaving for that island for four days, and thus the question arose what to do with those days. Remaining in Sira was out of the question, for although, in a commercial point of view, I am told that it is the most important Greek town; all that anybody can care to see of Sira is seen from the harbour. Perhaps I should mention that from the top of the hill on which the Roman Catholic Church stands, there is a fine view over the town; the harbour, which is full of all kinds of vessels, and looks very animated, and the blue Ionian Sea.

But then the way up that little hill is very steep, and the sunbeams strike down upon the streets paved with slippery stones, which makes the going up fatiguing, and the coming down difficult. Carriages cannot be used at all. The houses of Sira are all painted white, or of some very light colour, and look neat and clean, but the country around wants entirely the charm of vegetation. There are about a dozen trees planted round a little square in the town, which form the only promenade of its inhabitants. I saw no other tree or shrub anywhere on the hills around, so that the inhabitants know only by the higher or lower degree of temperature whether it is summer or winter; nothing else tells them of the pleasant changes of the " circling year." And what is worse still, Sira has no fresh water. This indispensable necessary of life, this great element of our existence, which I always thought belonged to every man like the air he breathes, as his birthright, is brought to Sira from a distance and sold like wine by the quart, and of different qualities; that fit for drinking being the dearest.

The town has no historical recollections, no antiquities, no art treasures, ancient or modern;

nothing but ships and warehouses, and stones, and a burning sun. We could not stop four days in such a place; that was evident. But where to go?

We committed a grievous error in the way in which we solved that question. Athens, with its glorious remains of antiquity was, so to say, at our door, being but ten hours' journey from Sira. But unfortunately there was at the same time a boat leaving for Smyrna, which would return in time for us to catch the boat for Crete; and so, partly from a childish impatience to see an eastern town, as if I had not been going to Crete and Constantinople afterwards; partly because I liked to spend another day with the excursionists, we went on board the "Germania;" had forty-eight hours of rough sea (twenty-four each way) two days at Smyrna, with what enjoyment I shall tell by and by, and lost the opportunity of seeing Athens, to which I could afterwards only pay a flying visit of a few hours on my way from Constantinople to Messina.

The only point of interest on our journey to Smyrna was Chio, where we arrived at daybreak, and which, illumined by the rising sun, was a glorious sight. The high mountains of the island look bold and stern, but they slope down to gentle hills covered with rich vegetation, and there, partly buried in woods of oranges and olives, lies the town. Ah! beautiful, unhappy Chio, so cruelly oppressed by the Turks, who fear the bold and daring spirit of its inhabitants, which has manifested itself so often in rebellion, and for which they have suffered so terribly.

From the consequences of the massacre in 1822, when many thousands were killed, sold as slaves, or fled the country, it has not yet entirely recovered. But seen from the steamboat, in the glory of the morning sun, it looked all smiling, and happy, and beautiful. As the men are renowned for their bold daring spirit, (an Ionian proverb says "A prudent Chiote is as rare as a green horse;") so the women of Chio are famous for their beauty and sprightly grace. Surely I thought Chio must be the birthplace of the great bard, whose glorious works still delight the world, and are imperishable, like the "everlasting" hills" that rise up there through the silver clouds into the blue sky. Here he saw men of such bold and adventurous spirit as those he describes so well, and women of such godlike beauty, that he could describe the immortals as if he had dwelt among them; and a mortal woman of such transcendent grace and charm as Helena. "May the cruel Turk be soon driven away from thy smiling shores," I prayed, when our boat left the harbour of Chio on our way to Smyrna.

From Sira to Smyrna we had some new travelling companions, among whom I must mention M. R—— and his wife, from Paris, on a journey to the interior of Syria, where M. R—— was going to complete the material for the continuation of his work, the beginning of which, published a few years ago, created so much sensation and controversy. Mme. de H—— the sister of the Archbishop, looked at him with no friendly eyes, and confided to me, that she feared with such a man some misfortune would happen to the vessel; and she cast suspicious looks at the sky, which at that moment was overcast and threatening. I thought of this again, when two months later I was told at Naples the following little story. It is well known that no people in the world are so fond of saints as the Neapolitans. They adore an endless number of them, and have "tutti i Santi" always on their lips. When M. R——'s famous book was first published, the Roman clergy (as other clergy have done on another occasion) drew the attention of the whole laity to it by preaching violent sermons against it. In Naples, as at some other places, they also read masses and held processions for the purpose of mitigating, by such pious practices, the evil that book might create. A Neapolitan peasant woman, who had not understood much of the sermon, besides the words procession and the name of R——, thought he must be some saint whose name she had forgotten, there were so many; how could she remember them all? So she put on her "vestito di festa" and lighted her candle, and when asked for what purpose, innocently said that it was in honour of St. R——! I wonder which would have amused the sceptical and learned professor most, if I had told him of the superstitious fears with which he had inspired Mme. de H——, or of his canonization by the Neapolitan peasant woman.

At Chio some Turks came on board; the first Mussulmans I had seen. One of them was a venerable looking old man, and as soon as he came on board he spread out a piece of carpet, took off his slippers and knelt down, his face turned towards Mecca, his hands lifted up in prayer. Another one, a young man, had a monkey and three bears with him. The monkey was large, the bears short, shaggy things. They danced several times to his music, which consisted of a monotonous noise, meant probably to be a song, accompanied by the beating of a tambourin. The beasts danced with their usual grace.

We arrived "saufs et sains" at Smyrna, and

the last few hours the journey was pleasant, for we had entered the Gulf and felt no more the movement of the sea. The colour of the water had changed from a deep blue to a bright green, and the vessel kept close to the southern shore of the coast, which was very lovely, being covered to the very tops of the mountains with rich vegetation of soft delicate colouring. Two mountains, called the "Two Brothers," had a sterner look, having bare rocky crowns; but the "Three Sisters," which are a little further on, were of a soft and gentle aspect.

The nearer we came to Smyrna the more animated became the Gulf with craft of different kinds. The small Greek sailing vessels having spread their white sails before the fresh blowing "Levante," the Eastwind, glided swiftly over the water, looking like some gigantic sea-fowl raising the waves with outspread wings. And then, at the foot of green mountains, in an emerald plain, among cypresses and olives, I beheld Smyrna, "The Amiable," "The Crown of Ionia," "The Pearl of the East." We landed; a giant boatman took most of our luggage on his back, and conducted us to the hotel. I had difficulty in following the large strides of the tall fellow, who walked apparently with perfect ease, barefooted, over wretched pavement, with a heavy load on his back, whilst I picked my way painfully over heaps of rubbish, sharp pointed stones, open gutters, and holes in the pavement. I looked around me and saw, to my utter astonishment, that what had appeared a paradise, was a dirty, wretched place, worse than I should imagine Whitechapel to be. I was quite horrified when we entered the hotel to think that we were going to stay in such a wretched place. And the room we were shown into was not much better than the appearance of the house had led us to expect. Whitewashed walls, not over clean, a very dirty piece of carpet, which I pushed with my foot at once into a corner of the room, and hard beds, a ricketty wash-hand stand, a sofa, and one chair, was all the furniture. As this was however, the best hotel in Smyrna, and no other room to be had, we were obliged to consider this charming apartment our home for two days.

When we were ready to go out I asked the Dragoman, as interpreters or guides are called here, to take us to some pretty street, when he answered, with a polite bow, "Madam, the pretty streets of Smyrna are like this," and what was this one like? A narrow, wretched lane, paved in such a way as to make walking a penance. In the middle of the street an open gutter, full of mud and abomination, heaps of rubbish, and refuse, over which I had to climb, deep holes which I must try to avoid. The smaller streets seemed to serve not only as thoroughfares but as workshops and stables. In one that was but ten steps from our hotel a cooper and his men were at work all day, and close by, I noticed at all times, a cow tied to a post, so I thought she had no other stabling. I wanted to see the beautiful Greek women, of whom I had read in Eothen; but it being neither Sunday nor fête-day they did not show themselves; of the few I saw none answered to the description of the author of that clever book. But there were few women of any kind visible.

In Corfu and Sira I had been struck with the almost entire absence of women among the people in the streets; in Smyrna I observed the same thing, although in a less degree, owing, no doubt, to the residence of a large number of Europeans. (The Greeks are not called Europeans in Smyrna.) The private houses of the upper classes, especially of the rich Armenians, looked very well indeed. The doors of most of the houses being open, one can look into them. They appeared neat and clean. In their gardens there were cypresses and orange trees, and the sweet smell of flowers. But we Western women, although we love our home, do not like to be locked up in it, be it ever so fair a house or garden. We want to go about for pleasure and for health, but to do that would be an impossibility in Smyrna.

Alas! I thought if this is "the Pearl of the East," I have no wish to see the beads. It is very old fashioned, I know, to find fault with any thing out of old England, and it is not "bon ton" to long after the English flesh-pots, but I must be honest, and therefore confess, that although I was very willing to be satisfied with the food, I sadly longed after English cleanliness and order.

One thing I remember however, with pleasure, that is the school for girls of the German deaconesses. It seems the abode of peace and piety, but without the restraint and superstition of a convent. Sister Mima is an able and excellent Directress, and the institution a blessing to the whole East. I went also and looked at the new railway station, which seemed an anomaly in a country where riding on horses and camels seems the most natural means of locomotion.

I also enjoyed my meals at Smyrna, not that they were particularly well cooked, but because we partook of them in company with Mr. R—— and his wife. She is pleasing and amiable; he does not seem either. But his conversation is decidedly interesting. All he says secures attention. He expresses his thoughts with great precision. He speaks almost as well as he writes, and that is saying a great deal. I was however, very glad when the time came for our boat to leave for Sira; although the weather was unfavourable and foretold a bad passage. The night was pitch dark with alternate showers and hail storms; the Captain told us that near Chio he was but thirty yards from another vessel before they saw one another. In Sira, the French steamer of the Messageries Impériales and several other smaller craft were driven ashore, but without serious damage. If the wind had not abated there might have been danger. There were on board with us more than two hundred poor Greeks, most of them beggars, that went on a pilgrimage to Tino near Sira, for a great fête of the Madonna there.

The Greeks are so anxious to go and adore the miraculous Madonna there, that even the Turkish Government took notice of it, and probably in order to propitiate the good will of the Greek subjects in Crete, placed a frigate at the disposal of the municipality of Canea, which had thus the means of giving a free passage to the many poor of the island who wished to go to Tino.

Those from Smyrna that were in our boat were all wretched and dirty-looking people. Many of them were very ill, and had undertaken this journey, hoping that the Madonna of Tino would do for them what doctors had not done. The cold pelting rain of the stormy night did at least for one poor creature what she thought of asking the Madonna to perform—it ended all her sufferings.

She was a woman of about thirty years of age and paralyzed. The doctor on board the "Germania," when he found how ill she was, had tried to bleed her; but circulation had already ceased, and she died about an hour before we reached Sira. This caused some delay in our landing. The Captain had to go on shore and inform the sanitary officers that a death had occurred on board. After some time, they took the dead body ashore in order to have it inspected. I saw the poor creature lying in the boat in which they had placed her, propped up with pillows and carefully covered, but her white face was visible, and the breeze played with her dark tresses.

About an hour after a boat approached and the cry of "pratica," meaning here "intercourse," was heard from it; and we were now at liberty to leave the "Germania" and go on shore. There was the usual noise and bustle and confusion, and quarrelling and fighting. We waited till it had subsided, and then we went at once on board the little boat called "Shield," which was to leave the same afternoon for Crete. It looked just like a common steamboat, only very small, but it was an enchanted vessel, which a kind fairy had sent to take me to fairy-land. There was nobody on board besides ourselves, the captain, and the crew, and some people on the foredeck. I had not been long on board, when I felt very sleepy. I thought it was because I had not slept the night before, but I know better now. That sleep came over me that I might not see the way into fairy-land, which people should only enter when the fairies send for them. When I awoke, after a long, deep sleep, it was morning, and I was in the enchanted island.

CHAPTER II.

CRETE, OR THE ENCHANTED ISLAND.

"Hier ruhn im Kranze
Von Blüth' und Frucht, als Zwilling
  Herbst und Frühling,
Doch Idas Scheitel strahlt im Silberglanze."

E. Geibel.

Is it not a dream, a delusion? Am I really in Crete? Shall I not awake suddenly and find myself at home, and hear the voices of my children? Those flower wildernesses, which people call here "gardens," those noble snow-covered mountains, they belong to fairy-land; and the strange crowd of people, and the curious little half clad black children that play on the sea-shore yonder, are they real beings of flesh and blood, or phantoms that haunt the enchanted island?

Thus I felt when first I came to Crete. My life here seemed so strange, so new, that it was like a dream. But when I awoke to it morning after morning, then that brilliant sky, and the flowers that grew beneath it, the deep blue sea, down upon which I had sometimes looked through the latticed windows of the Pasha's harem, the pretty little Circassian slaves, and the ugly black ones, in gay fantastic dress, that stood at the open doors, the strange sounds of the Turkish band playing on the old walls of the city, and the melancholy Greek songs of Leilà, the Pasha's daughter—all became a reality that neither dazzled nor confused me any longer. But they were happy days, those days in Crete; and when I think of them, it is as if I felt again the fresh breeze of the sea, and the balmy one that blows from the south; and wafts to us the smell of orange-groves in blossom, and of all the roses that bloom in the gardens of Crete, and I see the land and the sea smiling under the bright sun of the East.

There was no hotel of any kind on the island; we had therefore, accepted the invitation of an Italian gentleman residing there, who, when apprized of our intention to visit Crete, had asked us most pressingly to stay at his house in Canea, the principal town.

He expected our arrival on the 3rd of April, and came on board our steamboat as soon as it had anchored in the harbour of Canea.

There was no difficulty in identifying us, we were the only first-class passengers on board. After exchanging some kind words with Signor A—, and seeing to our luggage, we stept into the little boat which had brought him on board, and crossed the harbour. How strange and new a world it seemed in which I was; the town, the people, the sky, the sea, the very air I breathed.

What is that large white palace on the left side of the harbour? I asked. "The Pasha's Seraglio,"* Sig. A— answered: " and do you see that part of it which faces the sea, and where all the windows are covered by thick lattice work, that is the Harem." Not far from the Seraglio I noticed a row of large vaults. Sig. A— told me that they had been built by the Venetians, who used to keep their gallies in them. The fortress at the right hand of the harbour was also built by them. So were the fine strong city walls, on which I afterwards noticed in several places the sign of the Lion of St. Mark. We landed and wound our way through a crowd of strange looking people. They were Turks and Greeks in their national dresses,

---

* Seraglio means a palace. Harem means sacred, and is that part of the Seraglio which is assigned to the women.

and Africans with not much dress of any kind. The streets were decently clean, and would have looked almost cheerful if there had not been a great number of large dogs, with a wild, hungry, wolf-like look, who were lying everywhere on the pavement. Most of the houses round the harbour were coffee houses, the doors of which were wide open. In these open places, and outside the doors too, a great number of Turks and Greeks were sitting and smoking long chiboucs and hookahs; I noticed but very few people that wore the European dress. A walk of about five minutes brought us to the house of Sig. A—, a modest dwelling, although it was perhaps the best furnished private house in Canea. But if the floors were bare, they were faultlessly clean, and the plain bed and window curtains, were of a dazling whiteness.

Round the windows of my bedroom grew some pretty creepers, and the sky that peeped through this green frame into my room was of a brilliancy such as I had never seen before, and the air that streamed through the open window was so soft and fresh at the same time, that but to breathe was an enjoyment. Sig. A— was, as I said before, an Italian by birth. Chance had brought him, when a young naval officer, from St. Remo, near Genoa, to Crete, and fate had ordained that he should fall in love with the daughter of the Italian consul there, who made him forget his home, which he never saw again, for he gave up his profession and settled at Crete. He had been a widower now, poor man, for several years, his wife having died young, leaving him four little children and a wretched portrait of herself, which some roving dauber had made, which he however held in high estimation, and could never look at without emotion. Towards us he was the most amiable of hosts, and showed his pleasure in entertaining us in a kind and hearty manner. We found it difficult to remember under how many obligations we were to him, for he almost succeeded in persuading us that it was he who was beholden to us. His children were kind, good-natured and timid, and never more pleased than when they could be of some little service to me. The Genoese housekeeper, a tall, masculine-looking, middle-aged woman, who had a moustache many a young ensign would have coveted, did also what she could to make me comfortable, and appeared to feel over-rewarded for all her trouble by my listening now and then to her complaints against Canea and its wooden houses, the slovenly Greek servants, and the wicked Turks, the lean butcher's meat, and the coarse flour ; it was an endless catalogue of complaints, interrupted only by her praises of her Genoa, which, through the distance of time and space, appeared to her even more beautiful than it is. There all the people live in marble palaces, which have nothing of wood but the window frames and doors; the ladies wear only silk and velvet, and the large beautiful churches are covered with rich paintings. But if her praises were somewhat exaggerated, I must own that her complaints were not wholly groundless. The beef I found decidedly uneatable, as they kill only cows which are too old to give milk, and oxen too old for work. The mutton was of the very poorest quality, lamb and chicken only just eatable, but very inferior to what we are accustomed to. The people seem to eat a great deal of salted sardines, caviare, olives, and such like things. I did not care for them, and lived principally upon eggs, salad, and oranges, the latter of a size and flavour unknown in England. With Nicolo and Marico, the Greek servant boy and maid, I could however find no fault. It is true they wore no stockings, and I suppose Marietta, the housekeeper, did not accuse them without reason of having but a very slight feeling of the obligation of telling the truth, but then they were so nice looking, their dress was so picturesque, their manners so gentle and winning, that I could not help liking them.

We were a fortnight under the roof of kind Sig. A—, with the exception of the few days we spent on an excursion to Rettimo, and a pleasant, never to be forgotten time it was. I generally spent my mornings alone most quietly and happily at the little table, near my open bedroom window, reading or writing, and sometimes forgetting both, and looking dreamily into the blue sky, or at the fragrant flowers in the glass before me. For there were never wanting some flowers from garden and field to sweeten my room. The kind people with whom I lived finding that I was fond of flowers, supplied me abundantly with bouquets of such marvellous beauty, that to look at them and to breathe their fragrant odours gave me a lively pleasure, even now the recollection produces a gentle emotion, like the remembrance of some happy childhood's Christmas, or some moonlight walk in spring time, when the heart has just learned what love is. The wild flowers I gathered myself, and that I did so much astonished my host and his family. They thought it decidedly eccentric to gather wild flowers, put them into water, and look at them with pleasure, as if they had been garden roses or orange blossoms.

In the afternoon we always went out, either for an excursion on mules or for a long walk. I was very fond of a stroll round the old fortifications of the city, from which I could see the cheerful animated looking town, with its elegant minarets, and the blue sea beyond it—the fruitful plain bordered by the glorious chain of the Sphakistiki, meaning "white mountains," whose snowy crowns shone in the light of the declining day, and formed a picture more beautiful than anything I had ever seen or dreamt of. Here the Turkish band used to play in the evening. They sometimes performed European music, but their national marches and the hymn to the Sultan they played with more spirit and gusto, and the strange wild sounds seemed also to me more in harmony with the scene around.

The crowd of little black urchins that always congregated near the band also preferred the latter music. They stared sulkily, or with indifference at the performers when they played some of Bellini's or Meyerbeer's compositions, but as soon as they began some oriental tune the sulky look changed into a broad grin, which showed their white teeth; and their legs, arms and heads began to move about in a lively and droll manner.

They contrasted singularly with the grave and

dignified look of the Turks that were sitting or standing about, smoking cigarettes, or playing mechanically with a string of large beads in their hands. The Greeks that were present walked about engaged in conversation, which they accompanied with expressive movements of the face and lively gesticulations. The Turkish soldiers also assembled near, being called together by a flourish of trumpets. Before they dispersed they bowed several times low down, touched breast and forehead as if in salute, and shrieked out some barbarous word which means " Long life to the Sultan." Far apart, on a green slope, sat the Turkish women, with their children and black slaves. These women, wrapped in satin cloaks, their heads and faces covered by their white veils, the gaily dressed little children with their bright happy faces and dark sparkling eyes, the black female slaves in cotton dresses of the Turkish cut, and most gorgeous colours and patterns, produced altogether a charming picture. When we had listened for a while to the music we usually took a walk into the country. Our road led sometimes through lanes formed by high cactus and aloe hedges, or across corn fields where the corn (it was the beginning of April) was already beginning to ripen; over green meadows full of brilliant and beautiful flowers, or through cool orange and sombre olive groves, till we reached one of the many and beautiful gardens for which the island has been renowned in all ages.* Out of the snow-white foam lying on the breast of the azure waves which kiss the shores of Cyprus, rose Aphrodite the goddess of love and beauty, but Flora must have been born in Crete, or why should the flowers that bloom in its gardens have more brilliant hues and exhale sweeter odours than all the other flowers of our beautiful earth. Yet thus it is. I shall never forget the evening when I first entered through a humble gate in a whitewashed wall, the garden of Sakhir Bey. Then for the first time I knew why Eden was a garden, no splendid palace, but a garden with the sweet smell of flowers, with the shade of noble trees, and the sound of murmuring waters. Oh! thought I, that I might be allowed to dream my life away here, that that gate would shut out for ever the noisy bustling world.

This garden was very different from our gardens at home, nor was it the most beautiful of Crete,

* "Oranges, lemons, pomegranates, and all other fruits, are produced in the greatest abundance, and sold at the vilest prices. The gardens are rich and beautiful, and adorned with many plants unknown in other countries."— *History of Candia*, published in 1550.

but it was the first I saw there, and it made the deepest and most lasting impression upon me.

Art has done little, Nature prodigiously much. The flowers grow so luxuriantly, that man's hand cannot keep them in bounds. They grow high, intertwine, and intermingle; they stretch their long branches full of rich blossoms across the paths; they touch your shoulder and catch your veil, but they are wonderfully sweet and lovely. The scent of the orange blossoms and roses is so strong, that it has a physical effect upon your nerves, and gives you a feeling of unspeakable enjoyment and bliss. The son of Sakhir Bey, the happy proprietor of this little Paradise, received us most kindly. He was the first Turk I ever spoke to. At the beginning of our conversation, carried on in French, I felt a little embarrassed, for I remembered that he belonged to a nation that treats women as slaves, and seems to despise them as such. He however soon made me forget it, by his perfect politeness and courtesy. He told one of his gardeners to bring us fruits of different kinds, some of which I had not seen or tasted before, and when I left I carried away with me a bouquet as large as my hand would hold, and so sweet, that for days after when it stood in my room, I felt as if I were again in

Sakhir Bey's garden. I visited many other gardens, I saw the beautiful " Pine-tree Garden" of Hamet Bey, " the garden of the Red Country" belonging to Memet Bey, and the splendid one of Pasha Mustapha, but none that pleased me more than the first.

Far, far from here, they still bloom in the sun, and in the soft clear moonlight, those gardens of Crete! That my foot ever trod their flower-strewed paths, that my hand plucked their glorious roses, seems now a dream. The stately Bey alone walks them now, and at times when the gates are firmly closed, some veiled woman with slow measured steps, and dark burning eyes, followed by some black slave, whose ugly features appear the more repugnant in that world of beauty.

The day after we arrived at Canea my husband paid, as is customary in the East, a visit to Ismael Pasha, who is Governor-General of Crete. The history of this remarkable man is singular and romantic. He was born at Chio, of Greek parents, made a slave by the Turks when a boy of eleven years of age, and sold to a Turkish doctor in Constantinople, who taught him what little he himself knew of his profession, and employed him as an assistant. When Ismael had grown to be a young man, he showed so much talent and ability, that his master most justly thought his young assistant might, if he received an European education, become a competitor of the French, German, and Italian doctors in Constantinople, who were more frequently consulted, and better paid by the wealthy Turks, than the practitioners of their own nation. He therefore sent the young man to Paris, where he studied for five years. When he returned to Constantinople, he far surpassed his master's most sanguine expectations; and his great ability and success were soon generally acknowledged, and he rose in a short time to the dignity of physician to the late Sultan; and afterwards, when it was seen that his talents in other directions were equally remarkable, he became the Governor of Provinces. In Crete, where he has been for several years, he is respected and loved by all well disposed people. He encourages agriculture, makes roads, punishes crime, and judges justly. Under his mild and firm rule, the Greek inhabitants have almost become reconciled to the hated dominion of the Turks; and have petitioned the Sublime Porte to prolong his Pashalik. A few days after his visit, my husband received an invitation to dine in the Seraglio. The note of invitation ran as follows: " Le Gouverneur Général de Crête prie Monsieur

V. de lui faire l'honneur de venir diner chez lui, demain Jeudi, vers le coucher du soleil.

"Sérail, Mercredi."

I thought it quite a poetical and Oriental mode of fixing a dinner hour " vers le coucher du soleil ;" as however the Turks count their hours differently and in a way that is most puzzling to a European, this was perhaps the best way to prevent a mistake, for the sun sets at the same hour over the faithful and over the infidels. The latter flattering appellation is bestowed upon all who are not Mussulmans. The evening Mr. V. dined with the Pasha was not a gay one for me. Being tired after a long day's ride on a mule, I sat down at my open window looking at the moon. She shines much brighter there than in England, but it seems she exercises the same influence there as here ; I became quite melancholy and sentimental ; I longed for my children, and asked the moon to kiss them for me in their little cribs in England.

The next morning I paid my first visit to the Pasha's Harem. My husband conducted me to the entrance of the Seraglio, that leads into the Harem, the part of the palace occupied by the women, when an old grey-bearded Turk opened the door from the outside with a large key, and locked it again as soon as he had let me in. I must confess I did not quite like the fashion in which that stern old man with daggers and pistols in his belt, had closed the outer world behind me, and I cast " a longing, lingering look behind" at the strongly barred door.

I slowly crossed the yard towards another door I saw before me; and at which the old man had pointed before he locked me in. It opened at my approach, and I was met and saluted by several women in the Turkish costume; the first I saw without veils, who led me up a wide staircase to a landing that resembled a large saloon. At the top of the stairs I was received by the Pasha, who led me into a spacious apartment with divans all around, but no other furniture. He left me there alone, but returned almost immediately, accompanied by two ladies, the one a young and pretty timid looking girl, in a rich Turkish dress; the other a middle-aged lady, in plain European clothes, with a pale face, and two large piercing black eyes, and who, after the Pasha had named his daughter, was introduced to me as Mdlle. Elizabeth.

The windows of the Harem are hermetically closed, allowing no air and but little light to enter, this is admitted through the doors principally, which lead into spacious halls or terraces, overlooking the court-yard, or little inner gardens, and are seldom closed. At the open door of the apartment in which I was, appeared a crowd of slaves, most of them so young as to be mere children. Some were richly, all gaily dressed The prettiest of them was a little Circassian, of about twelve years of age, the favourite of her mistress, who was dressed in pink silk, and had a wreath of artificial flowers in her hair. But I have not spoken of the mistress yet. Although her father is a Greek by birth, the daughter was of the Turkish type. She is short, and would be considered too stout with us, but has only the " en bon point" indispensable to a Turkish beauty. Her round face wore an expression of kindness and good humour, and was remarkable for a pair of fine large intelligent black eyes. Her dress was entirely composed of green silk, trimmed with crimson velvet. On her head she wore a little round black hat, evidently an European importation, for it was very much like those worn in England; it had a fine white feather fastened to it with a diamond ornament; and a brooch with the miniature of her father, in a setting of diamonds a Queen might have coveted, sparkled on her breast. This splendid ornament had formerly contained the portrait of the late Sultan, who had given it to the Pasha.

When Ismael Pasha had introduced me to the ladies, he left us alone, and the first awkward moments over, my visit became a very interesting one, Mdlle. Elizabeth addressed me in English, which she had acquired at the American Missionary School at Athens, and like most Greeks, possessing a great talent for acquiring languages, she spoke it well and fluently. When however I heard that Mdlle. Leilà could understand and speak a little French, I preferred speaking to her without the aid of an interpreter, and gradually she overcame her bashfulness, and entered into conversation with me. I had often been told, and it is unfortunately to a great extent but too true, that Turkish women, even the wives and daughters of Pashas, can neither read nor write. How much was I therefore surprised and pleased, when I found that Leilà knew not only her own language thoroughly, but Greek and French as well. The Pasha, a most enlightened man, has given to his daughter an education, which under the difficulties with which he had to contend, is truly wonderful. She had studied Turkish when still a child, with the present Caimacam, or under Pasha, of the town of Candia, a man of great learning; and Mdlle. Elizabeth, of whom I shall speak more by and bye, had taught her Greek and French. She possessed several books, among which I remarked a Bible in Turkish, and " Paul et Virginie." Mdlle. Elizabeth asked me if I wished to hear Leilà sing and play, as she was very musical, and had had good instructions at Constantinople. Of course I said that I should be delighted to hear her, and we then went into a room where I found a good piano from Vienna, which was not much out of tune. Leilà sat down and played with a clear fine touch, a very good arrangement of " God save the Queen." This was a pretty compliment. She had played but a few minutes when her father came in. He told her to play a Turkish march, which she performed with perfect execution. She played also a Mazurka by Schulhoff, and one or two other pieces. At last her father desired her to sing some Greek songs. Words and music were both perfectly unintelligible to me, but sounded very melancholy; and that feeling so took possession of me, that I found it difficult to prevent its being observed. There sang the poor little bird who, though the bars of her cage were gilded, and her master gentle and kind, was a prisoner for life. She will of course, before long, change her master, and be married to a man, who let us hope will love her, but who will never bestow upon her more than a trifling part of his presence.

But at least she may hope to be his only wife, as Mdlle. Elizabeth told me that the Pasha will not give his precious little daughter but to a man who will marry only one woman. The Pasha himself has had but one wife, by whom he had three children; the eldest is the wife of Kadri Bey, then comes Leilà Hanum, and Foad Bey, a fine boy of fourteen years of age, the father's hope and pride, who is receiving an excellent education.

When Leilà had finished, I warmly expressed my delight and surprise to the father, who also seemed much delighted. I daresay he had never listened with more pleasure to Lelià's music than when he saw it approved and admired by another.

Of how much pleasure and happiness this abominable system of seclusion deprives these people. We all know, that however much the fortunate husband of a beautiful clever and virtuous wife may love and admire her, his love and admiration are again and again stimulated by seeing her inspire similar sentiments in others. He cannot become indifferent to her charms, while he witnesses the impression they make upon others. But suppose this paragon to be locked up, and

her husband never to see her except in a tête
a tête. She may be faultlessly beautiful and ex-
quisitely dressed, he is accustomed to it, and it
strikes him no more. The wonderful intelligence
of his firstborn, the droll sayings of his little one,
which every father delights in showing off before
his astonished friends, all these and numberless
other joys, he must forego. The life with his
family loses all charm, it becomes—but no, I will
not describe what it becomes, for that is disgusting. The desire of the Turk to separate his wife
from the rest of the world, goes so far, that he
even dislikes to hear her mentioned. Mr. A—
our host, told me, that he once inquired of a husband after the health of his wife, who was reported
to be very ill, when the Turk, who usually was a
polite and amiable man, at once looked dark and
suspicious, while he answered with a scowl, "What
is my wife to you? Do you know her, that you
ask after her?" Leilà seemed much pleased with
my visit, offering me three times refreshments,
consisting of sweets, coffee, and sorbets, which
Turkish ladies do when they wish to honour their
visitors, and having them served at long intervals,
which shows the desire on their part to prolong
the visitor's stay. She asked me to come often,
to bring my work or book, and stay as long as it

pleased me. I visited her several times, because I liked the lofty airy rooms, and to sit on the broad divan under the window, and peep through the lattice-work down upon the boundless sea, that eternal image of fetterless freedom, and see the slaves glide past, or sip the coffee they offered me. But though I had some book in my hand, I did not read much, but like a regular Turk dreamt a few hours away, thinking of the fate of the poor girls around me, and thanking God that I was born a free woman in a Christian country. There were in this Harem none of the horrid male slaves that disgusted me so much in some Harems I afterwards visited; Ismael Pasha, a wise and high-minded man, does not suffer them in his household.

And now I must not forget to say a few words more about Mdlle. Elizabeth Konta Xaki, whose acquaintance I made at my first visit to Leilà, for our intercourse did not end there. I saw her several times afterwards, and she contributed much to make my stay in Crete interesting and instructive, being always ready to give any information I wanted regarding the country and its inhabitants, and being better fitted for it than anybody else.

Mdlle. Elizabeth of Crete, for that is the name

by which she is generally known, is a very remarkable woman. She was born in Crete, but received her education in Athens, and lives in an Eastern Island with the manners and habits of the West. She walks and travels about alone, protected only by the respect all have for her. Her learning and extensive knowledge would excite attention in any place in Europe; it is therefore but natural that in an island, where few women can read or write, she is the wonder and astonishment of all the inhabitants, and occupies quite a distinguished and influential position. The rebellious Greek mountaineers, the terror of the Turkish Government, respect her, and have more than once consulted her, and listened to her advice, for they know that she is a warm patriot, while the Pasha seldom fails to ask her opinion on the measures of reform he wishes to introduce, as he knows how well she can judge of their importance and utility, and that she is not hostile to the Government of the Sultan. She has written more than once to the Grand Vizier in Constantinople, and her communications have always received the attention they deserve. She has a straightforward, fearless mode in stating her opinions, which contrasts singularly with the servile manner of her compatriots. She lives alone with her aged mother, and a female servant, in a little house, in a narrow street, but her room, overlooking a little garden, is large and pleasant. Over her writing table hangs a pleasing portrait of our Queen, which was given to her by an English friend. Some interesting antiquities in marble and terra-cotta, found in Crete, are the only ornaments of the room.

Her large book-case is well filled with books in classic and modern languages. I, who am not at all learned, looked with awe and veneration at the long rows of Greek and Latin authors, which evidently stood there not for ornament, but had been often read and well used. To me she became a most interesting and valuable companion, and I shall always remember, with a feeling of interest and kindness, Mdlle. Elizabeth of Crete.

The first excursion we made was to Galata, a Greek village about two hours ride from Canea, where M. Malatachi, a friend of our host Sig. A—, had a delightful country house. He had taken a great liking to us, for what reason I cannot tell, for we could speak to each other by signs only, or through an interpreter, which is a tedious way of carrying on a conversation. However, he evidently liked us much, and pressed us to pay him a visit in Galata. On the morning fixed for the excursion, M. Malatachi came with a long train of mules and servants to fetch us. My mule was a splendid white creature, with a scarlet bridle, and a rich carpet spread over the wooden Turkish saddle, I mounted it, feeling very proud and elated. One of M. Malatachi's handsomely dressed Greek servants walked or ran, as the case might be, by the side of my mule, so as to be at my service if required.

I looked down upon him with the dignified air of an Eastern Queen, fancying myself very much like one. My husband observed my look, and broke out into a loud laugh, which I considered very mal à propos, and which rudely destroyed the pretty illusion. He, as well as Sig. A— and his two eldest children, were all well mounted; and in high spirits we set out. O blessed climate of Crete! There was no need to fear rain or cold, nor was the heat oppressive, but the air was delightfully warm, genial, and balmy. The roads were bad, of course they were. Where would have been the fun if they had been like "Rotten Row."

The Turkish saddle, in spite of its handsome covering, was not very comfortable; but who could think of the saddle, whilst looking at the glory of the sky and earth, or mountain top, and into the flowering valley.

When we were about a mile out of the city, we came to the mud huts where the poor lepers live. These miserable creatures lay or crouched before their doors, and stretched their mutilated hands out towards us, begging for alms. My husband threw a few piasters among them, but I turned my face away, for they were frightful to look at.

The sad impression these poor wretches made upon us however quickly vanished, like a mist before that golden sunshine, which made all nature around us at this moment look smiling and beautiful. Our way led through cornfields and vineyards, up steep hills, and down green valleys, across clear murmuring brooks, and through an olive grove, where the trees were very old and large. Four men could not have encircled with extended arms, some of their old hollow curiously twisted trunks.

When we reached Galata, the little children in the streets called their parents, who rushed to the doors and windows to see us. The Turks are not at all curious, or if so, they hide their curiosity most carefully, for they never seem to look at a stranger. The Greeks, on the contrary, have much curiosity, and show it with the greatest naiveté, following you about, and examining all you have and do. "You are at the house of your slave," said M. Malatachi bowing, and putting his right hand on his breast, when we had dismounted and entered his house in Galata. It is delightfully situated. The view from the large stone balcony, over hills and valleys, on to mountains and the sea, with the little island St. Theodore, is indescribable. I spent a delightful hour there quietly by myself. Not being able to speak the language of the country, may occasionally prove an advantage. Our interpreter being engaged with a long conversation on the value of land and the produce of the country, between M. Malatachi and my husband, I could not talk with our hostess, who seemed a kind, but very timid lady. She interrupted my musings only by sending me a continued round of sweetmeats, coffee, sorbets, and lemonades. Then came the dinner; " What is mine is yours," said our Greek host, when we sat down to dine. For so primitive a country as Crete, it was a sumptuous repast, of which however, neither host nor hostess partook. It being Lent, their dinner consisted of vegetables, olives, &c.; but they looked very well satisfied with their frugal meal, and seemed pleased to see us enjoy the good things they had provided, and if they could not eat with us, they drank our health more than once, a compliment which we of course returned.

We left Galata towards five o'clock in the afternoon. A boy ran in front of our cavalcade, carrying a splendid bouquet M. Malatachi had given me, and escorted us back to the very door of Sig. A—'s house. "Your visit has been like a refreshing evening breeze after a sultry day," said M. M. when he took leave of us. This poetical way of speaking, which is a common mode of expression in the East, there sounds natural and pretty; I felt however to the last rather puzzled how to reply to those high-flown compliments. The people there have another peculiarity which pleased me still more. Whenever for instance I mentioned my children, they would say, "May the great God protect them." " A long life to them all." " A happy return to them," or something like it.

We also spent a delightful day with Sig. A— and M. Malatachi at Plantagna, so called on account of the noble old plane trees that grow there, round each of which a gigantic vine grows, covering stem and branches. A fine clear mountain stream, of which this favoured island has many, flows through the valley, and near its banks, under the finest of all the noble trees that shed their shade over the flowery grass, we halted. It was the same tree under which Mehemet Ali, the famous

Pasha of Egypt, had once dined and rested, when he had come to Crete to chastise the rebellious Greeks. We spread our carpet, dined and rested, walked about and rested again, till the declining sun reminded us that it was time to think of our return to town. We had gone by an easy road along the sea shore; we returned by one that lay inland, and very different from the first. It was a regular Crete road, a stony path, up and down steep hills, through brooks and across shaky bridges. We had not calculated that we should not be able to ride so quickly on this road as we had done on the other; so it happened that the sun set when we were still at least an hour and a half's ride from the gates of Canea, and they are always shut an hour after sunset. We made our tired mules step out as fast as the roads would allow, but it was a hopeless case, we could not have arrived in time. Sig. A— who knew my great horror of the very ugly and dirty black people, " Arabs" as they are called there, who live in mud huts and dirty tents outside the town, proposed that we should ask them to take us in, whereupon I declared with great energy and decision, that for my part I should prefer to spend the night with the pretty little white lambs on the hill side, whose bells were heard tinkling in the stillness of the night, rather than with those ugly black sheep. Sig. A— therefore promised that I should be driven to neither extremity, but sleep comfortably in my own bed. All the inconvenience resulting from our being too late would be that we should have to wait at the gate of the town till one of the soldiers had fetched the keys from the Pasha's palace, where they are kept after the gate is shut. But we were spared even this trifling inconvenience. That is the advantage of living in a place like Canea, where M. Malatachi, who is a judge, Sig. A—, and we, two distinguished foreigners, were of great importance.

The guard of the gate knew that we left Canea in the morning, and had not yet returned, so they kept the keys for half an hour, and we entered without delay. What a difference to living in London, where like a drop of water in the sea, the individual is undistinguished, lost in the immensity.

The longest and most interesting of our excursions was the one to Rettimo, which is two days' journey from Canea. Unfortunately the weather, which had been faultless all the week, changed the day before we intended to start. The blue sky became overcast, and a strong tramontane, as the north wind is there called, was blowing. As however it did not rain, we started on Saturday, in hopes of a change for the better, as people said a strong tramontane was a very unusual thing in April, and occurred only in December or January, and could not therefore last.

The Pasha had given us his Capo Cavalliero, which means the head of his guards, as an escort, which he does when he wishes to honour the visitors of Crete. He was, as became so great a personage, a very imposing looking man, and had so many splendid pistols, daggers and knives in his scarf, that he looked as if he alone could have killed a whole regiment of brigands. Besides, the Pasha had kindly sent us one of his black servants, who, he told us, *understood* a little French, having been in the service of Prince Napoleon during the Crimean war. If the Pasha had said that Sali could *speak* a little French he would have been more correct, for he did talk French a little; but was it that I did not speak with a pure Parisian accent, like Prince Napoleon, or like a governess that has been six months abroad; certain it is, he never understood what I said to him, and gave the most extraordinary answers to some of the very simple questions I put to him. But, as with Mrs. Blimber, of whom Mr. Dickens says that she was not learned, but that she pretended to be so, and that did quite as well, so with Sali; he pretended to understand French, and that was quite enough. We got every thing we wanted, and more than we wanted; and if I wished to know the name of some place we passed, by pointing at it with my hand the intelligent Greek muleteer that was walking by the side of my mule knew at once what I wanted, and told me. However Sali was useful in his way; he rode behind us, looked picturesque, and gave to our cavalcade a more imposing and eastern look. The Capo of course led the party. He rode a little beauty of a horse. Close behind him followed my husband on a mule, I came next, also on a mule; Arif, another guard the Pasha had sent, rode behind me. He carried, besides his pistols, &c., an immense long gun over his shoulder, of which I was rather afraid, knowing that it was loaded; for he prepared once or twice to shoot some bird with it. However, he did not shoot me nor any bird, or robber either, none of the last coming within range. Then followed the mules with our luggage and provisions, and Sali concluded the train. But cruelly cruel one gets in the East. One cannot keep on being sorry that a poor man runs by your side, while you sit comfortably on your mule, which, as a matter of course, takes the only narrow little bit of road, while the man jumps over stones and through thorns. For four miles, between Canea and Suda, the road was comparatively speaking good; it has lately been repaired, because the Sultan has declared his intention to visit Crete ere long, and he will land at Suda, which has the best port in the island, and the only safe one in rough weather; but after passing Suda we came to the mountains, and then began the Stradaccie, as our host Sig. A— had most properly called them. Our mules however did wonders, picking their way through the stones, walking up and down steep steps in the rock, in a marvellous manner. Had I, after having travelled for a little while in this way, been told that we should go up some perpendicular wall, I should have believed it. If our way was strewn with stones instead of flowers, they at least grew in perfection on each side. Wild roses, of singular bright colours, and many other strange and beautiful flowers, which I do not mention, for the simple reason that I do not know their names; and shrubs and trees as strange and new to me. I only recognized here and there a familiar face, as gorse, rhododendrons, and wild fig-trees. Among the flowers there were more old friends, buttercups and daisies, dandelions and wild thyme, which used at home to tell that spring time had come. The stones and rocks were also strange and curious. What they were I do not say, for the very same reason that I did not tell the names of all the flowers. Ah, whoever wants useful information about Crete must go there himself, or send somebody else. I can describe but little of what I saw, although my eyes were wide open, and my heart had unlocked all its chambers, and rejoiced that " this beauteous world is made so bright." I should however have liked to press many of the flowers, only my supply of blotting paper was limited. Not being of a botanical turn of mind, I had not brought any for that purpose with me, and could not supply the want, as there was none to be got on the island. After three hours' ride we arrived at Armenos, a hamlet, where we halted, and Sali and Arif unpacked some of our provisions. I never enjoyed a lunch more. It consisted of cold chicken, hard boiled eggs, oranges, and Turkish coffee, and we partook of it in the shade of a splendid plane tree, on the borders of a clear murmuring stream. On leaving Armenos, the country became wilder, and the roads even worse than they had been; an ascent of about half an hour, the whole country around was strewed with fragments of rocks. It would have looked terribly wild and desolate, had not the wild flowers and plants covered and hidden a great deal. As it was, it reminded me of the Turkish cemetery at Canea, the pieces of rock resembling the gravestones, which tumble and lie about there in all directions. But if the going up was difficult, the going down was a great deal more so. We came at last to a point where we had to dismount and clamber down for about half an hour, for the road was very steep, and turned and twisted about at sharp angles. However, about three hours after we had left Armenos, we arrived safely at Xopoli, where we intended to spend the night.

Xopoli, a Greek village, is the most desolate place I ever saw. It gives one the impression of one great ruin. Having been built entirely of stone, it has not the mean wretched look of a Turkish village, but partakes rather of the melancholy grandeur of a ruined castle. To judge from the remains, it must once have been a large place, and was like so many others destroyed by the Turks, after they had butchered the Greek inhabitants. A few of the very poorest of this once glorious race still find shelter in these ruins. I noticed here and there a door or a shutter, and a thin column of smoke rising from some chimney. But when we rode, and afterwards walked through the village, we hardly met a creature.

But thanks to the great kindness and civility of the Pasha, who had the day before sent a messenger there, we found a shelter prepared for us, and although a most singular kind of a lodging, I did not wish it different. The house in which we were going to spend the night was the only one that had preserved a second story, standing also on the highest spot of the village, it rose like a tower above the others. Stone steps led on the outside of the house up to a little stone landing, and from thence into a kind of loft. Two mattresses, and a few pillows, covered with clean white linen, had been laid on the ground, they represented the beds, the chairs, the sofas, the tables, and every thing else. There was however, hanging in a large old fire-place, a little brass lamp, of an antique shape, intended to light our apartment, if the moon should refuse to do so; which seemed likely, as the sky continued to look threatening, and the wind was high. But if there was not much to be seen in the room, the look out was splendid. Through the little open door we could see the hills and mountains, on which light and shade constantly changed with the passing clouds. Through the solitary little window which had a shutter, but no panes of glass, never having been able to boast of such unnecessary finery, we overlooked a deep valley stretching northward as far as the sea, which we saw at a distance. Our host, although a Turk, showed us every possible attention; if only in consequence of the Pasha's orders, or because he did not absolutely hate all Christians, I cannot tell, for I could not talk to him. We dined at twelve o'clock Turkish time,* which, as we were in the middle of April, is about half-past six o'clock, and our room being rather dark, we had a carpet spread on the little stone landing outside the door, and took our meal there. I call the landing little, for it was only four feet square, without any kind of railing round it, and there we sat perched up high; high, for the hill on which the house stands slopes rapidly down in front of it. But a glorious dining room it was. At our feet, a valley full of cornfields and olive woods, beyond it, noble mountains rising into the clouds; yea, here and there lifting their venerable snow-covered heads, glowing in the evening light, above them; and in the distance to our left the rolling sea. We sat there a long time after our simple meal was over, and watched the effect of shades

* The Turks count their hours from sunset, which is always 12 o'clock; when the next day begins.

and moonshine on the landscape, and the stars that shone forth as the clouds swept away. It was very still all around us. I heard no sound but that of some hidden brook flowing over stones and pebbles; but now and then the wind sighed past us, and made the olive trees murmur.

All at once I heard a sound that seemed strange and yet familar. It was the song of the cuckoo of Crete. It resembles the call of our cuckoo, in so far as it also consists of two notes; but they are not the same notes, and he rests longer on the last than our cuckoo does. He sang a long time, I heard him still in my sleep. Of other birds of any kind I heard or saw little on my excursions through Crete. A few large black creatures, which I took for ravens, a flock of what seemed a kind of pigeon, swallows, and sparrows, who there as here made as much noise as they could; but I heard no sound that resembled the song of the lark, the thrush, the blackbird, or the nightingale. Altogether the island seemed to me poor as regards animal life. Horses and mules are very beautiful in form, but extremely small; so are the cows and oxen, which are not larger than a fine donkey is with us. The sheep and goats are also quite diminutive creatures. The little lambs are lovely, but when they get a few months old, they look very lean and miserable. After a night which had not been very refreshing, for I was not quite accustomed yet to that kind of night accommodation, we set out early in the morning for our second day's expedition.

Our way led us through the valley I had looked down into from our castle tower at Xopoli, towards the sea-shore. When we had reached it, my guide jumped up on the horse behind Sali, and the party put itself into a canter, which with little intervals lasted two hours; we only fell into a walk when sometimes the shore became very shingly, or when the sand was very soft and wet, which the mules particularly disliked. They seemed never to mind how steep, or stony, a road was, but on damp and muddy places they looked with great suspicion, and could only be coaxed or driven across. After two hours sharp riding we came to a little river that flows into the sea. Mustapha led us to a point where we could cross, and then under the broken arch of a ruined bridge we halted and breakfasted with a hearty appetite. What however somewhat disturbed our enjoyment of the meal was, that Sali told us, now would begin the bad roads. After what we had gone through, to be told that the bad roads were but coming, was rather hard. However, as like to Küsnach "there led no other road" to Rettimo, we set out for it, when we had rested ourselves. And the reality was far worse than my gloomiest anticipations had pictured. As I had never thought of trying a ride on the top of Milan Cathedral, I could have formed no idea of the road from Petres (our halting place) to Rettimo. Like the top of that famous building, we were in a forest of stone. The sea, the rain, the air, had worked almost as elaborately as the mason and sculptor. And through this forest of stone and rock, up steep mountains and down again, sometimes high above the sea, then again so near to it that the spray wetted the feet of our mules, we had to pick our way for two hours. To make matters worse still, a heavy shower came on, and in order to protect ourselves a little against it, we had to turn our backs to it, and halt till it passed over. Happily the high wind prevented the shower from continuing, so after a little while we were able to proceed on our journey. My husband, who had put on his waterproof, and tied a handkerchief round his ears, over his battered wide-a-wake, to prevent its being blown away, looked anything but dignified, which however, under the circumstances, was of small consequence.

Our guides, on the contrary, pulling the capuch

of their cloaks over their heads, looked if anything more picturesque and imposing. The worst part of the road lasted about two hours. That seems a short time, not worth mentioning, but any one who for instance has crossed the Channel in very rough weather, and been wretchedly sick all the time, will know that two hours may seem very long. However, our mules carried us safely along, and by and bye the road, although still very bad, was on comparatively level ground, which made it much less trying. For the last mile or so the road was good, and thus we reached Rettimo. It lies on a promontory, which ends in a cliff, on which a fortress is built that looks strong and foreboding. There are no gardens here like in Canea, the shrubs and trees here and there are stunted, and grow in a horizontal direction, as trees and shrubs will do near a sea-shore which is exposed to high winds. One solitary palm-tree is an exception; it stands in some little garden in the town, and rises high above the houses, waving its graceful leaves. " What is this town here for, in this stony wilderness, on a rocky coast, with but a small harbour, which can be entered in fair weather only?" I asked our host, M. G—. He told me that behind these mountains are fruitful valleys full of olive-trees, the fruit of which the peasants bring to Rettimo, where it is made into oil and soap. We visited one of the many soap manufactories in Rettimo; the soap was very nice and pure, and I heartily wished that it had been more extensively used in the island, instead of being exported to Constantinople, Trieste, &c.

M. G——, the English Vice Consul, in whose house we lived, and who received us with great kindness, is an Ionian Greek. He spoke Italian, and one of his sons had also a slight knowledge of that language, which enabled him generally to make out what we said, though he seemed to have great difficulty in replying. My husband, however, persisted in saying that M. Pietro's want of fluency in speech, arose from another cause than from a want of knowledge of the language. He said he was sure I had made a conquest, and I am inclined not altogether to disbelieve that assertion, for he certainly seemed uncommonly fond of being in the same room with us, and whenever he was there he stared at me with a mixed expression of kindness and wonder in his face, which was so ridiculous that it cost me a supreme effort to suppress a smile whenever I looked at him. When he heard that I was fond of flowers he brought me some twice or thrice a day. Where he got them from I cannot tell, for they are not so plentiful at Rettimo as they are at beautiful Canea.

M. G—'s wife, daughter, and daughters-in-law understood nothing but Greek. I could, therefore, only speak with them by signs, and as one can convey but very simple ideas by that mode of communication, we did not tell one another much. They were dressed in a way that was a mixture of primitive simplicity and gorgeous finery. With a plain cotton dress, and a handkerchief tied round the head, they would yet wear splendid diamond ear-rings, pearl necklace, bracelets, etc. There was the same incongruity observable in their houses, which were wanting in many of what seem to us the very first and indispensable comforts of life, while the beds had gold embroidered counterpanes. With the children I got on better than with these ladies. I won at once the heart of a little boy to whom I showed my air-cushion, and who never tired of filling it and then letting the air escape again. He would abandon this delightful occupation only in order to look through my opera-glass; but, of course, using it the wrong way, so as to make things that were near appear far off and small, which he seemed to think much more interesting than bringing distant objects near.

But it was not only my air-cushion and opera-glass which excited the curiosity and wonder of the little and big children at Rettimo. Every thing I had and wore seemed to astonish them— my kid gloves, my straw hat and feather, the cut of my dress, my diary. They saw me once or twice write down some little note into it, and seemed to watch the operation with a kind of awe. I, for my part, was surprised at the absence of many common things. I have already mentioned that I could not buy any blotting paper; they told me that for a pair of kid gloves one would have to send to Smyrna, which is a forty-eight hours' sea-voyage, four times the journey between London and Paris, and I found it even difficult to get a few hair-pins. The wary Greek shopkeeper of whom I inquired for the latter article, as he could not serve me with it, offered me instead, to my great amusement, a whole chest of Holloway's pills and ointment at a greatly reduced price. The enterprising quack had actually sent a chest of his valuable medicines to Rettimo, but the natives evincing no inclination to take them, the Greek hoped he might get rid of his stock by selling it to me, thinking, as he told me, that all English people took these pills as regularly as their dinners or suppers. Why had not Mr. Holloway read in the "Museum of Antiquities" that extract from a history of Candia, published in 1550, where they say:—"The primitive name by which this country was known was Aëria, which was given to it on account of the temperature and salubrity of the air, and from the fertility and abundance which reigned in the island. It is, indeed, most temperate, insomuch that the inhabitants have much less need of medicine than in other countries, and consequently live to a great age—occasionally to one hundred and twenty or one hundred and thirty, and the author confirms having seen one who, by his baptismal records, proved himself to be one hundred and thirty-four, and was then in the possession of all his faculties." What will become of the pills in so provokingly healthy a country? Probably they will be eaten by the ants which abound there in summer; with what effect upon their digestion, I cannot conjecture. I am sorry to say that the weather, which had not been very favourable on our journey to Rettimo, became, after our arrival there, very rough and stormy indeed. The people there said they never remembered such a Tramontane (north-wind) except in December or January. The gale blew for twenty-four hours, the sea had become exceedingly rough, and now and then we had a pelting rain. Under these circumstances we found Rettimo anything but a pleasant sejour, and the worst was that as long as this weather lasted the Lloyd steamer, which was to take us back to Canea, could not be expected to arrive. When on the next day the wind had abated a little, and the weather was altogether finer, we went out for a stroll to the sands. The sea was still very rough, and we looked disconsolate towards the horizon, feeling very much like two poor shipwrecked creatures on a desert coast, and evincing a strong inclination to quarrel with every thing and every body. All at once I cried delighted, like Enoch Arden, " A sail, a sail," it was however no sail, but what was a thousand times more welcome still, the funnel of a steamer. We saw however, at once, that it was not the Lloyd, but the Greek steamer, as it came from the opposite direction from which the former was expected; still we conjectured that if one could come the other would also arrive ere long. We hurried to the port to see her come in, and to get our letters, which we knew were on board. The fine vessel rode gallantly on the waves, and seemed to rock but little. It approached the entrance of the harbour: now it will stop, I thought, and in half an hour I shall have my letters, when coolly and proudly she passed on, finding the sea too rough to venture the disembarcation of either letters, merchandize, or passengers. My dear longed-for letters went to Candia, and although it is but forty miles from Rettimo, they could not return before the lapse of a whole week, when the steamer would bring them back. Ah! one must be patient and in no hurry in Crete. The forty poor passengers for Rettimo, who as I afterwards heard had been on board the Greek steamboat, must have found that out. They too were left at Candia, and had to wait there a week till the steamer returning from Sira brought them to their destination.

Our impatience drove us again to the shore after dinner, to look out for the Austrian steamer, but we spied for it in vain. The weather, however, became clearer and pleasanter as the day declined, and shortly before sunset all the clouds that had hung over the island vanished, and then appeared, as if by magic, the mountain giant Ida shining in the evening light.

We had intended to make an excursion from Rettimo to Mount Ida, and visit the "Cradle of the Gods,"

> " Rea la scelse già per cuna fida
> Del suo figliolo * * * * *"—*Dante.*

and try to discover the sources of the infernal streams,

> "Lor corso in questa valle si diroccia;
> Fanno Acheronte, Stige e Flegetonta;"

but this plan could not be carried out on account of the weather. I felt a pang of regret that I had not been able to reach it, " it seemed so near, and yet so far."

But the sun set, the rosy light on the snowy mountain top disappeared, and we had to return to our quarters with the disagreeable impression that we might have to sleep another night at Rettimo. I longed to be in Canea again, which was much the pleasanter place.

We sat up later than usual, and had only just gone to bed when our host knocked at our door and told us that the steamer was in sight. We dressed quickly, and then our host and his son, of whom I have spoken before, conducted us to the Marina. The boy carried in one hand a bouquet of roses he had given me in the morning, in the other a little lantern, for the streets of Rettimo are not lighted up, and after dusk, every one is obliged under pain of imprisonment, to carry a lantern about with him.

When we arrived at the harbour I saw the

lights of the steamer at what seemed to me a great distance out at sea.

A row in a small boat at night, and in a rough sea, is not at all a thing I am particularly fond of, for I am not of a romantic turn of mind; I dislike adventures, and have, above all, a great objection to being drowned.

However, in Rettimo I could not remain, so I must try to reach the steamer. When in the boat, I clung tightly to my husband, who promised to take care of me. How much were we surprised when the young man with the lantern and the flowers boldly entered the boat after us, for I had been told by his brother-in-law that M. Pietro was afraid of the water, having once had a very bad passage to Smyrna. But in answer to our remonstrances he said, as well as he could in his broken Italian, that he would see us safely on board.

When we were out of the harbour, and the little boat went up and down the high waves, he called out every time a new wave came, "Non paura, non paura!" if to encourage me or himself I cannot tell. But he did me a service by coming; it amused me so much that I forgot my fear while laughing at my husband's good-humoured jokes at the poor fellow. When he had given me my roses, and we had shaken hands and thanked him, he left with his lantern. We watched the little light as it danced up and down on the waves till it reached terra firma, and knew then that the kind soul had no more need to call out " Non paura!"

We arrived safely at Canea; and two days after Marietta packed my trunks while I went to pay a farewell visit to Leilà, at a country-house in Kaleppa, where the Pasha had removed his family during my absence from Canea. I drove there in the Pasha's carriage, the only vehicle of any kind on the island, and which resembled somewhat the Lord Mayor's coach.

On Monday, the 17th of April, we left Canea and paid a flying visit to Candia, the ancient capital of the island. We walked through the town, which is a desolate place—ten times too large for its inhabitants. Grass grows in all the streets, and the very dogs seem more lean and hungry here than elsewhere. The fine massive old Venetian walls that surround the harbour and town have been cracked by earthquakes, and they seem unable to resist the general decay. There are many palm-trees in Candia whose graceful forms rise up amidst the ruin and desolation which surround them; and beyond the town, as in Canea, one sees a chain of snow-covered mountains.

It was noon when we weighed anchor, and the steamer left. I remained on deck as long as I could see the island; the sea in the blaze of the mid-day sun was of a brilliant blue, the sky showed all shades of it from a deep azure over head, to a pale milky-white on the horizon. And thus, encircled by sea and sky, lay like a giant emerald the enchanted island to which a kind fairy had led me to dream away a few weeks that had passed like so many hours. Farther and farther it receded. Now, I can no longer distinguish the snow-covered mountain-tops from the clouds above them; all becomes misty and indistinct. I shut my eyes for a little while, for I have strained them in looking so fixedly. I open them again—it is gone like a dream. I see it no more! the enchanted island has vanished.

CHAPTER III.

CONSTANTINOPLE.*

"Along with the barbarous Turk
Where woman has never a soul to save."
                                        THOMAS HOOD.

GOETHE says in his journey to Italy: "Thus it was written on my leaf in the Book of Fate, that on the twenty-eighth of September, 1786, towards five o'clock in the evening, I should see Venice for the first time." So important and momentous —so much like an event—appeared also to me

---

* It is with great diffidence that I print this chapter, as I am conscious that so short a stay in a place so strange, and to strangers, in part so little accessible as Constantinople, could not enable me to form any competent judgment of the people that inhabit it. I intended, therefore, to confine myself merely to a description of their outward appearance and manners without drawing any conclusions or forming any judgment. I find, however, that I have not been able to keep my good intention. May the reader take these remarks for what they are worth, and pardon the errors into which I have surely fallen.

my entry into Constantinople on the twenty-first of April, 1865.

It was about seven o'clock in the morning when we saw the seven towers that mark the beginning of the town. I had been already some time on deck, pacing it with a feeling akin to the emotion with which I used to sit when a child in some theatre, before the rising of the curtain, expecting to see a Christmas Pantomime. And, as in that happy age, the red and blue fire, and the lovely fairies in pink tarlatan with silver gauze wings, far surpass our greatest expectations, so, although I had formed no mean idea of what I was going to see, did the sight of Constantinople far surpass all I had ever imagined. After we had passed the Seraglio Point and neared the harbour, the city appeared to encircle the sea and close around us. It was not so much the beauty, as the grandeur that surprised me. Genoa "la superba" and even glorious Naples appear but small in comparison to the wide extended sea and the mountains that tower above them; but Constantinople appears great in proportion to the surrounding scenery—a gigantic town. Immediately after we had passed the "Seven Towers" the mist that had till then obscured the horizon disappeared, and now the grand picture lay before us in a clear transparent light. It was a most exciting, happy moment. Round our boat crowds of porpoises were gambolling in the water in the " maddest, merriest " manner; over our head we saw innumerable flights of birds of passage coming from the south, and bringing the spring to Constantinople. At the very moment our boat entered the harbour all the Turkish men-of-war lying there, having all their flags hoisted, began to fire a splendid cannonade. The people around me said they were firing because it was Friday, which is the Turkish Sunday, and the Sultan was just going to the Mosque. That may have been the case; but at that moment I felt as elated as any Sultan can feel, and it seemed to me those guns were firing only to express the joy and wonder of my heart at what is certainly one of the most wonderful sights in the world. I shall not attempt to describe it; that has been done by far abler pens than mine, and even they have failed in conveying to their readers any adequate idea of it. In fact, I believe it is a hopeless undertaking. As no description can give to an Esquimaux an idea of the warmth and brightness of the sun when its rays make the waves of the Bosphorus and the Gulf of Naples appear a sea of gold; or a South

American, who had heard nothing but the shriek of parrots and cockatoos, could never imagine what the song of the nightingale or lark is like; so one must have seen Constantinople and Scutari, the Golden Horn and the Bosphorus to know what they are like, as they resemble nothing else on earth.

Everybody knows that Constantinople seen from the sea, is the grandest and most beautiful town in the world; it is also a well known fact that as soon as one puts one's foot on shore, the picture changes entirely. But I must confess that after Smyrna, and the towns of Crete, I did not find it so wretchedly mean and dirty as I had expected, although the houses of Pera (the European quarter) are insignificant, and the wooden palaces of Stamboul not at all imposing. I never had much time to look at them, for the people that move through the streets, and that seem a series of strange, interesting, and beautiful pictures attracted all my attention. I advise all painters who are at a loss for subjects to go to Constantinople; one stroll along the great street of Pera, or through the bazaars of Stamboul, will supply him with subjects for years, so picturesque and beautiful is the life that moves around him. The first figure you see is the Kaïktchi or boatman, who in his kaik, the most elegantly shaped, and most neatly ornamental boat in the world, takes you ashore. With his bronzed face, his athletic chest and shoulders, in his thin silk shirt, that leaves his muscular arms and chest uncovered, his whole dress consisting besides this shirt of a red fez, and a pair of white pantaloons, he presents a most striking appearance; but you have hardly time to look at this new and interesting figure, when another one attracts your attention, it is the Hammal, or porter of Constantinople, who carries your luggage, which consists perhaps of two large trunks, a hat box, a dressing bag, wrappers, umbrellas, etc., all at once on his back. This human beast of burden is dressed in a light brown flannel suit, trimmed with black braid. He is often an elderly man, with a mild venerable face, and bent almost double under the weight on his back, looks the personification of the words "In the sweat of thy brow thou shalt eat thy bread." But there are gayer pictures in the streets of Pera. You step aside to let a carriage pass, that is all gilt and glass, and that comes rattling up the streets. A child would mistake the coachman for a prince, so splendid does he look in his gold embroidered coat. The pavement, even in Pera, is not good enough to allow a carriage to drive quickly, so you have full leisure to look at its inmates. The crimson curtains are half let down, and through them a magic light falls on the picture within. Generally the carriage is occupied by three or four Turkish ladies. They are always young, and all look beautiful ; old ladies it seems have no carriages to ride in. The mothers of Beys and Pashas stop at home, dressed in old calico gowns which they exchange for some rich attire on extraordinary occasions only. These young Turkish beauties wear gossamer veils so thin and transparent, as to hide no beauty of form or colour, while they just soften any little defect of either. Under this thin veil, face and neck show off to great advantage, and the jewellery they wear, and the gay colours of their satin cloaks, seen in the soft crimson light of the carriage, produce a very charming effect, unsurpassed even by our beauties, when they drive crowned with flowers, to the Princess of Wales' Drawing-room. I think it is in these carriages that Turkish ladies look best, even better than in the Harem, where however, when they are well dressed, gracefully reclining on the divan, they often look very beautiful. Only those who are above the middle size, and they are few, look well standing. None walk gracefully, not even those that have exchanged the sock and clumsy slippers, usually worn, for French chaussure. This however is considered no fault in a Turkish lady, who would be almost ashamed to walk well, as it would prove that she had often used such vulgar exertion. Having a whole host of female slaves at her command, a Turkish lady moves about but little when in the Harem, which she never leaves except in a carriage. The women of the middle and lower classes however walk as badly as the ladies, which appears to be occasioned in a great measure by their mode of sitting. They shuffle along with their toes turned in, wearing large yellow boots, over which they often have slippers of the same colour. You seldom see a really pretty face among them. I believe beauty has a market value in Constantinople, and the women know that very well, and wont marry a poor man if their face can buy them a rich one. We must however not judge them too harshly on that account. Marriage from love is out of the question in a country where it would be scandal for a man to say that a lady is beautiful. He must never have seen her face, nor have exchanged a word with her before she is his wife. He values nothing but beauty in his wife, she looks for a rich Harem, jewels, carriages, and a handsome compensation in case he sends her away. The women of the middle classes, who have of course no carriages, ride sometimes on horseback. They sit like men, and are accompanied by some black or white man servant, who runs behind the horse, and carries his mistress' slippers and parasol. These Amazons do not look particularly pretty or graceful, but the men on horseback are splendid. A Bey or Pasha, on a fine Arab horse, especially if he is an old man, and still wears the national dress, is a sight worth seeing. Horse and rider look as if moulded in one form, so firm and gracefully sits the rider in his saddle. Many of the horses are splendid, and seem gentle as well as lively, but now and then I saw a vicious one among the horses of the cavalry, that kicked with both front and hind legs, and frightened me in the narrow crowded streets of Stamboul. Yet I never saw any accident in consequence. The Turkish soldiers have a bold martial look, but in their dress they want entirely the neatness which European discipline requires of the soldier. The body guard of the Sultan looks magnificent. They are perhaps not such fine men as our horse-guards, but their dress is far more picturesque and imposing. But I forget that I intended to take you up the great street of

Pera, to our hotel. Well, all I have hitherto described you may have seen before you have taken many steps in that crowded thoroughfare. Who is the next person that passes you? A Circassian with his high fur cap, and his row of cartridges across his chest, leading a pretty child of ten or eleven years, with soft brown melancholy eyes. He is taking her to the slave dealer, unless he attract in the street the attention of some rich Turk, or Turkish lady, who will perhaps there and then buy the child and take her away.

The little Turkish children appeared to me anything but what are vulgarly called "little Turks." There are numbers of them in the streets, on the steamboats, and in the Harems, but I seldom saw a child in a real fit of naughtiness or passion. In their miniature dressing gowns of cotton, wool or silk, as the case may be, but always of most gorgeous colours and pattern, they looked funny little objects. The little girls in the Harems were sometimes pretty.

But what are those strange, wild figures, surrounded by a crowd of people coming slowly up the street? They are leading bears along to some more retired spot than the high street of Pera, where the bears and their masters dance together; a strange performance which the men accompany with a monotonous kind of song and beating of a tambourine. They look as uncouth and wild as the shaggy animals they lead along, but not more so than the shepherds you meet a little further on walking before their flocks of sheep and lambs. These wear a waistcoat and trowsers of undressed sheepskin, and a sheepskin hangs down their back as a cloak. Their long black hair falls over their shoulders and partly hides their faces. They carry long sticks in their hands, that look almost like the stems of young trees, and are of all the strange and wild figures you see perhaps the strangest and wildest.

What a contrast they form to the handsome Greek lady that now passes you. She is dressed in the latest Paris fashion, which is however modified just a little in accordance with the irresistible liking of all inhabitants of the South for gayer colours. Goethe observed this love for bright colours in Italy, and with his usual intelligence seems to have discovered at once a reason for it. What he wrote from Naples, on the 29th of May 1787, he might have written from Constantinople in 1865. He says: "The many coloured, variegated flowers and fruits, with which nature adorns itself here, seem to invite man to adorn himself and all that belongs to him with the brightest colours. Whoever can afford it decorates his hat with ribbons or flowers. Chairs and drawers in the poorest houses are painted with flowers, the carriages are scarlet with gilded ornaments, &c. We consider generally the love of gay colours vulgar and barbarous, and such it may become in certain conditions ; but beneath a very clear blue sky there really exists no very bright colour, because nothing can vie with the splendour of the sun and its reflexion on the sea. The brightest colour is softened by the powerful light, and because all colours, such as the green of the trees and plants, and the yellow, brown and red of the ground, act with full power upon the eye, the flowers and dresses harmonize with it. Everything seems desirous to become somewhat visible under the splendour of sky and sea."

If the Greek lady be the gayest figure in the crowd, the Arab woman is the most dreary and dismal. She is so entirely enveloped and thickly veiled, that but to look at her gives one a feeling of suffocation. The Turkish veil at Constantinople is a pretence, the Arab veil a reality. How the women can breathe or see through it is a wonder to me.

These are but a few of the strange and picturesque figures one meets on a walk through a street of Pera or Stamboul; there are many others, priests in a variety of dresses, Persians, Chaldeans, Jews, and some so strange and new, that like the flowers of Crete, I do not know their names, nor where they come from, nor what they mean. There are of course also some very disgusting sights; the dirty beggar that importunes you, the wretched lunatic with his shorn head uncovered, who touches your arm, the deaf and dumb boy that begs with hideous noises, the nasty dogs that in a torpid kind of dose lie about in the streets, and worst of all the cripples, that expose their deformed limbs in order to excite your pity. But as I always turned away from these wretched sights, I will not remember them here.

If this long description of a walk through Pera should seem tiring it is no wonder, for it is a long steep hill that leads from the Custom House where you land to the Hotel in Pera. Apropos of the Custom House, I must relate a little incident that happened to us when we arrived at Constantinople, and which well characterises Turkish Custom House administration. When the officer had minutely examined all our trunks, dressing-bags, etc., and had looked with great suspicion at my pincushion, the use of which he could not understand, and tried to open it in order to see if it contained any contraband, he discovered in a small basket half a dozen oranges, which kind Sig. A— of Canea had insisted upon my taking with me. These were seized, and the Turk asked us to pay five piastres (10*d*.) duty, when, to our utter astonishment, the dragoman of our hotel gave him one piastre (2*d*.), which he took and was thankful.

To walk up to the hotel in Pera is, as I said before, very tiring, for the hill is steep, the pavement bad, and there are no footpaths; still it is vastly preferable to driving. Those gaily-painted, gilded carriages have very bad springs, and on the pavement of Constantinople and across the wooden bridges they shake one to such a degree, that I felt if the human body was not grown together mine would surely have fallen to pieces. Men are much better off in that respect, they can hire a nice little horse, which may be found everywhere, and at a moderate price, while even a short drive always costs from fifty to seventy piastres (10*s*. or 12*s*.) There is one other kind of conveyance for women, that is the sedan-chair; it is not a cheap mode of transit, as you can go no distance under 6*s*. or 8*s*.; but the men carry you along quite as quickly as the carriages, and the movement is not unpleasant. These sedan-chairs are much used by the stout Greek and Armenian matrons. I did not notice that Turkish women used them, they seem to be of a sociable character, and like to go out in sets of three or four, and therefore ride in carriages.

A few days after our arrival we went the usual round of sight-seeing, in company with several other persons staying at the hotel, who all profited by the special permission which must be obtained before one can visit some of the places of interest in Constantinople. Our companions were all English; and I am sorry to say there were several of them with us who made themselves conspicuously ridiculous. One promising youth, measuring in his slippers at least five feet ten inches, wore a knickabocker suit like my little boy of seven, who has lately rebelled against this dress as too childish, declaring his determination to wear trousers; and, although it was as cold as on a March day with an easterly wind, and no more sun than shines on a bright November day in London, he had, in order to protect himself against the sunstroke, a large white handkerchief twisted round his wide-awake, which looked like a turban out-of-fashion. For turbans are quite out of fashion in Constantinople, where the red fez has been almost exclusively adopted as a head-covering. Another of the young men of our party had a pair of very small slippers which, when entering a mosque, he used to put over his large boots, of course with the heels down. They covered only half of his boots, which offended one of the Turkish priests, who told him through the dragoman to take his dusty boots off, but the proud young Briton refused to do so, and very nearly brought us all into trouble.

The sights of Constantinople are so far interesting as they are different from those of all other European capitals. Their novelty was the chief attraction they had for me. We saw them all in one day, which proves that there are not many.

We first visited the garden of the old Seraglio, whose situation on a gentle hill, sloping down to the Sea of Marmora, is one of the most beautiful in the world. There are large numbers of fine cypresses and plane-trees growing in masses there, almost like a forest, which gives an air of perfect solitude and retirement to the garden, although it is surrounded on two sides by one of the largest and busiest towns in the world. The beautiful old Seraglio that formerly adorned this splendid site was burned down a few years ago. It was then the residence of what are called the

"Imperial widows" of the late Sultan. These unhappy creatures are never allowed to leave the precincts of the palace that has been assigned to them as a residence, but must mourn, in perfect retirement, the loss of their late lord till death ends their existence. There is a rumour that one of these Serailee Hanum (that is the title by which they are distinguished), in order to get a chance of escape from her prison, set it on fire; but this is, of course, a conjecture only. The Dowager Sultanas inhabit now another large palace situated in the same garden, and I looked at its latticed windows, when it was pointed out to me, with a feeling of unspeakable pity.

There are in the same delightful locality some pretty Kiosks of the Sultan. One is called the Library, which did however not contain more books than a well stocked schoolroom in an English country house. We visited three mosques: the beautiful one of Sultan Sulimani, Sultan Achmet's, which has six minarets, and Aja Sophia, the grand old church, the very carpets of which look venerable.

The look-down from the high gallery into the nave, which was well filled with worshippers, was most interesting. The wretched little glass lamps, with which the Turks light up their mosques, are excessively ugly and out of keeping.

The Hippodrome now no more resembles a Roman Circus than Trafalgar Square does. Every trace of the ancient structure has disappeared, and the square is surrounded by Turkish mosques and houses. The large obelisk, that stands in the middle, shows however that this was the site of the splendid Hippodrome which was adorned by an infinite number of the finest Greek statues in marble and bronze. The famous horses of Lysippus, which once stood here, I remembered to have seen over the portals of St. Mark in Venice.

The least beautiful, but not the least interesting sight, is the gallery where the costumes of the Janizaries are exhibited. Most persons will remember that this Turkish soldiery, the formidable opponents of all progress and civilization in the Turkish Empire, the terror of the Sultans and the tyrants of the people, were burnt and massacred by thousands in the year 1826, by order of Sultan Mahmud II., who probably, in doing so, conferred an inestimable benefit upon the nation. A large number of lay figures, representing the principal functionaries of the household of the Sultan, the officers of the Janizaries, and the Janizaries themselves, who were not obliged to wear a uniform, stand there in the very dresses these people used to wear, and which are the strangest costumes the barbarous taste of a wild and haughty people could invent. They look a ghastly host now. I don't know that I ever felt more uncomfortable than during the time I found myself in their company. I would not stop a night alone in those galleries, not for all the treasures those terrible looking men possessed when alive.

I gladly turn my thoughts from this "dread abode" to the more cheerful life of the Bazaars of Stamboul, where you can buy sparkling diamonds and golden slippers, and all the "perfumes of Arabia." There is little besides the unavoidable atta of roses and embroidered slippers to tempt a not over acquisitive disposition. Ladies that are fond of diamonds can get them cheaper there than in London or Paris. But then one does not go to the Bazaars only for the purpose of purchasing at the stalls, every one of them is a new and striking picture. The principal figure in it is now an old grey-bearded Turk, who still wears his national dress, sitting on his carpet or reclining on his cushion, smoking his chibouque. He hardly changes his comfortable position, when your dragoman asks him for some article you want, and only rises if he cannot reach it while reclining. Or it is a lively black-eyed young

Greek, who spreads out before you as you pass his stall, a gold embroidered table-cover, or holds up some bright glittering beads, in order to excite your desire to purchase; or it is a long bearded Jew, in his oriental dress, that begins to talk to you in English, French and German, all at once, and offers to sell you every thing you can possibly want at the lowest possible price. What different figures are these from the London shopmen in their eternal black coats and white cravats, and the young shopwomen, their companions, in their everlasting black alpaca dresses, always standing behind the counter, even if there is nobody to serve.

The workshops, which like the stalls of the Bazaars are quite open towards the street, are also interesting to look at. You see the tailor cutting out his work, the cooper making barrels, the turner at his work, the coppersmith, the baker, the pastry-cook, &c. &c. Whenever the work allows it the workmen sit, and they do not look as if they laboured very hard.

As I wished much to visit some Harems in Constantinople, and see a little more of the Turkish women, my husband, in order to gratify my wish, procured for us introductions to some people of note, and took me to the Pashas and smoked chiboques with them, although I know he would have much preferred to take a kaik, and go to Bujuk Dere, or the sweet waters of Europe with me; for a row on the Bosphorus, or the Golden Horn, was what he most enjoyed at Constantinople. Before we visited the Pashas in Stamboul, I paid however my promised visit to Mme. Conemenos, the Greek lady, whose acquaintance I had made on the steamboat from Corfu to Sira. She was staying with her parents in Yeni Keui on the Bosphorus, where M. d'Aristarchi, her father, has a beautiful palace, a present of the late Sultan's, under whose reign M. d'Aristarchi, who is brother of the Prince of Samos, filled high offices of state. I remember my visit to this amiable family with great pleasure, for in going to Yeni Keui, which is one of the prettiest villages on the Bosphorus, I saw the beauty of that unrivalled spot for the first time. I spent a whole day there, and never was tired of looking on the beautiful scenery around, sitting near the window of some cool airy room of the palace, or walking through the shady and flowery garden that rises in terraces high above the blue waters of the Bosphorus.

The very next day we paid a visit to Omer Pasha, and were of course interested to see this great soldier of the Turkish Empire. He spoke with my husband about the Turkish army, agriculture, and horse breeding; to me about his two little children, a little girl of fifteen months, and a baby boy, who was then a few weeks old. These are his only children, besides a married daughter. He spoke with apparent regret that these children should have been given to him so late in life, and said that he could not hope to see them grow up, but as in spite of his advanced years, and a slight indisposition of which he complained, he still looked a fine man, I told him to trust in Providence, which might spare him still for many years. We parted after a visit of two hours, mutually well pleased I think, and with a promise to renew our acquaintance in London, which he intended visiting in the course of the summer. I did not enter his Harem, as his wife had been so lately confined, and could not receive visitors.

As Omer Pasha is a German by birth, and Ishmael Pasha is of Greek extraction, it was only when I visited Sami Pasha, that I knew I was with a real Mussulman, and I think it was partly for that reason that the visit to his house in Stamboul interested me more than the others I had paid. Sami Pasha, ex-Minister of Public Instruction, and member of the Privy Council, lives in a fine old mansion in Stamboul, which is separated from the bustle and noise of the city, by large court yards and gardens which surround the house on all sides. The house itself is one of the oldest and finest in Constantinople; the halls, and rooms, and staircases, are to an English eye very spacious, and the reception room, which is entirely of finely carved and richly gilded oak, and commands a splendid' view of Stamboul, is very beautiful.

Sami Pasha is quite an old man, with a very intelligent look, and the manners of a courtier. He has been Governor of many provinces, and seemed pleased to hear that he was still remembered at Crete, where he was Governor at the time the turbulent Greeks threatened a new insurrection, which his moderation and firmness had prevented from breaking out. He had years ago visited England and France, and was interested in all that concerned those countries. He had known many of our statesmen personally, as Sir Robert Peel and Lord Aberdeen; he inquired after Lord Palmerston, and seemed pleased that his Lordship, of whom he appeared to be a contemporary, was, like himself, still in the enjoyment of health and vigour. Although a member of the Privy Council, he holds no longer any special office, preferring quiet and retirement. He told me that his time was now entirely devoted to study and reflection, and that he was just then writing a treatise on morals. I had expressed a wish to see the " ladies of the house." I could not in this case ask to see his wife, as I knew he had two legitimate ones ; it is not often the case that Turks have more than one wife, partly I believe because it entails a large expenditure, each lady having entirely separate households, with their large suites of apartments, and numerous male and female slaves and attendants. After I had been announced to the ladies, a son of Sami Pasha, a young man of about seventeen years of age, with pleasant, courteous manners, led me into the Harem. All the doors that lead into it had been unlocked, perhaps in order not to shock my western prejudices, so that we walked freely into the ante-chamber of the Harem, where I met the first Hanum, who, looking rather embarrassed but not unkind, conducted me to another room. She was a stout lady of about thirty-five years of age, the mother of the young man that served us as interpreter. She was dressed in green silk, now the fashionable colour among the Turkish ladies, and had a many-coloured handkerchief, in a not unbecoming manner, wound round her head. I had just time to answer the questions these ladies generally ask, viz., how many children I had, their sex, ages, etc., when another lady entered through the open door, who seemed to be very nearly of the same age as the first, and who was dressed in exactly the same way, as sisters often are in England. She sat down on a divan opposite us, and I had to answer very nearly the same questions, when Sami Pasha joined us, and introduced his children to me. Both ladies have many children, among those of the younger there was a very pretty little girl of about three years of age, who, with her blue eyes and fair silken hair, might have been taken for an English child.

The Harem of Sami Pasha is very splendid, as becomes his rank and station. The windows, all overlooking the inner garden, are unlatticed, which was pleasant to me. The little stands which hold the Turkish coffee-cups were set with diamonds. All the slaves, and there seemed to be a very large number, were well dressed, some in silk, others in muslin, and they wore much jewellery. Most of them were Circassians, and, although no such great beauties as they are reported to be, were good-looking, comely young women.

The ladies received me with great courtesy,

offering me as a sign of good will, first sweets and coffee, then lemonade, then coffee again. The younger of the wives, who seemed pleased at my taking particular notice of her little girl, asked me to let her know that I had returned safely to England, and had found my children well. Of course I have complied with so kind a request, accompanying my letter with the photographs of my children. Sami Pasha had said before we left, "you must go and see my son's collection of antiquities;" and as we had already heard from others that it was the finest collection of the kind in Turkey, which, however, need not say much, we profited by Sami Pasha's offer, to announce our visit to his son, and went to see him the next day. Suphy Bey received his education at the Court of Mehemet Ali, the great Viceroy of Egypt, and is now a Privy Councillor like his father, and a man of great influence at the Sublime Porte, but he has never left the sacred ground of Islam, and is a thorough Mussulman. He speaks but very little French, and the first thing he offered me was a pipe, when I declined it, he asked if I preferred a cigarette, but even that I was obliged to refuse.

His collection of antiquities, is no doubt very splendid; but old Turkish coins have very little interest for me, as I understand nothing about them, but at the Greek antiquities I looked with pleasure.

I know that his Harem is one of the largest in Constantinople, but I was sorry afterwards that I had asked Suphy Bey to introduce me into it. His Harem is a palace, entirely separated from the house of the Bey, and in order to reach it he led me through two gardens, and the black slave who keeps the keys of the Harem had to unlock several strong doors before we could enter. We waited some time, and the Bey had, it appeared to me, dispatched several slaves before his first Hanum appeared to receive me. She did it with a face of chilling coldness; and, sitting down at the farther end of the room, addressed no other word to me than a polite inquiry after my health. The Bey smoked a chiboque, which a little girl, his daughter, had brought him; and there reigned an awful silence. At last the Bey rose and left the room; he returned after a few minutes, which had seemed to me terribly long, leading by her hand a lovely girl of about sixteen years of age, whom he introduced as the daughter of the proud lady opposite me, and who looked as if she entered the room " sorely against her will." She was by far the most beautiful woman I had seen in the different Harems, but she had the same expression of cool disdain in her face, that was so repulsive in the mother.

The father led her to a piano that was in the saloon, and she began to play. But the instrument was woefully out of tune, and never had the Turkish music sounded more discordant and barbarous, so that I could not express any approbation, and merely thanked her, when she had finished. Soon after I had been served with coffee, which was as bitter as wormwood, I rose, saying to the Bey that I did not wish to trouble the ladies any longer, being in fact anxious to bring this very unsatisfactory visit to a speedy end.

When I was again alone with my husband, I asked myself if I had any right to feel angry, or even annoyed at the cool reception these ladies gave me; placing myself in their position, I thought that I had reason to be surprised rather that they had abstained from absolute rudeness towards me, and had preserved at least the forms of politeness.

Should we like our husbands to receive ladies in their own apartments, and when it pleases them, only to bring those visitors for a quarter of an hour to see us, talking with them all the time in a language of which we do not understand a word, and then leaving us again alone, locked up, a prey to jealousy and envy? Really one need not be a Turk, under such circumstances to feel tortured by those ugly passions. Ah, I can forgive almost anything to the Turks: I will not condemn them for having erased the sign of the cross from the portals of Santa Sophia, for having made a powder magazine of the Parthenon, or for having slaughtered the Christians; but one thing I cannot forgive that they consign their own women to a life of idleness, ignorance, and immorality, and to a premature death. For Turkish women, who were healthy, strong girls at twelve years of age when they still enjoyed some liberty, die by hundreds of rapid consumption between the age of eighteen and thirty, in consequence of this unnatural, unhealthy mode of life. I advise all ladies that go to Constantinople, especially if they are under thirty years, (which however was not the case with me), and good looking, (and what woman under thirty does not think herself so), if they wish to visit a Harem, to do so in company of a lady who can speak Turkish, and thus serve as an interpreter. They will be more likely to be received kindly by the Turkish women, who will enter more freely into conversation with them if the husband be not the interpreter.

So poor in attractions for us was Constantinople in spite of the prodigious riches with which nature has endowed it, that we thought a fortnight too much to spend there. One fine morning therefore, we took the steamboat for Brussa, to which place we had a pressing invitation from an amiable and hospitable German family, residing there.

Our boat, which had left Constantinople at eight o'clock, arrived at Modagna towards two in the afternoon, and we found a carriage waiting for us, which after shaking us about like refractory cream that is to be turned into butter, set us down with a headache and backache at Brussa. But the next morning these ills had passed, and then I enjoyed my stay there so much, that I count the few days at Brussa among the pleasantest of my journey.

Brussa, the ancient capital of Turkey, lies in a fertile plain at the foot of Mount Olympus, which rises stately and imposing out of the plain. The town is of a thorough Turkish character. The houses are all of wood, the streets narrow, but they are cleaner than those of any other Turkish town I saw; and there are fine Mosques with elegant minarets. The Mosque of Sultan Mahomet, standing on a hill, especially pleased me, on account of its lovely situation. The little outer court with its fountain, which for the purpose of ablution, is found before every Mosque, shaded by noble old trees, is one of the most lovely spots I saw. It is cool, shady and quiet in the extreme. In Brussa the Turks still wear the real ancient costume; the large turban, the long dolman, trimmed with fur, the wide Mameluke pantaloons, the broad scarf, and rich arms.

Our ascent of the first plateau of Mount Olympus was splendid, at least so I thought, when I was safely down again. Till then, I confess, I did not find it quite so pleasant. Although I had become somewhat accustomed to bad roads on our excursions in Crete, I still thought those of Mount Olympus very terrible. They are narrow paths, fearfully steep, rocky and stony, leading often along precipices, or through thick woods, where the branches grow so low, that you are obliged bring your head to a level with your horse's to keep it on your shoulders. When I had gone up a little way, I did not wonder that our kind host and hostess, M. and Mme. S—, had not accompanied us; very few people would care to go up twice. Although the view is splendid, it is obtained at a great sacrifice, and can be enjoyed almost as well from a lower point, which can be easily climbed on foot. Mlle. Lina the daughter, and M. Charles S—, the brother of our host, had however joined us, and here I found how true is Schiller's word; "Den schreckt der Berg nicht, der darauf geboren," for both seemed to mind the roads very little. Mlle. Lina, every now and then, would draw my attention to some particularly beautiful view, which to look at from the giddy height we rode along, made my head turn. I could do nothing but look at the road and my husband; trembling lest horse and rider should go down some terrible precipice, for the roads were sometimes such, that I thought a false step of the horse would be immediate destruction of horse and rider. Our guide was a terrible Turk, looking as stern and calm as fate, in which he, like all Turks, had no doubt a blind faith. He took no more notice of us than if we had been in London or anywhere, except behind him. I am persuaded if one or two of us had fallen, and broken our necks, he would have taken no more notice, than he did of the stones that the feet of our horses now and then sent rolling down the precipice. He rode a wretched little horse, which besides himself, carried our shawls and provisions, but he looked perfectly at his ease. I suppose if he had broken his own neck, he would have met the unalterable decree of fate with the same stern, calm look.

But if I have not forgotten the bad roads, I

remember also with pleasure, the pleasant hours we spent on the plateau, from which rises the snow-covered summit of the mountain. On the plateau the snow lay in the shade of the trees, while the loveliest Alpine flowers grew in the sunshine; white and purple primroses, of a large size, pleased me especially. After we had rested, we wandered about, and except for the snow and the Alpine vegetation, we might have forgotten that we were on a high mountain, as there was no view of the world below. Shortly before one reaches the plateau, the view is splendid, extending over the mountains, the Lakes of Apollonia, and Nicæa, the Gulph of Gimlek, the town of Brussa, and the beautiful plain surrounding it. We saw, while we were on the plateau, a large vulture, and in descending, an eagle rose slowly and majestically out of a deep ravine. High up it soared, my eye followed it as long as it was visible, and I wished for "the wings of an eagle." We saw another interesting sight. We passed through a burnt forest. All the large trunks stood erect, but the bark had peeled off, and they looked very sad in their nakedness.

But what I remember with the greatest pleasure in thinking of Brussa, is the amiable family which received us so kindly. Mme. S—, is one of the most charming and amiable women I ever had the good fortune to become acquainted with. Although highly intellectual and accomplished, she lives contentedly in what I should call banishment, entirely devoted to the superintendence of her household, and the education of her daughters, who seem worthy of such a mother. Lina, the eldest, is in her simplicity and modesty so fascinating, that my husband, who is not in the habit of speaking in a poetical style, did so in speaking of her, and called her " a violet," while I thought her younger sister Annichen, very much resembled the bright wild roses that grow like her, round the foot of Mount Olympus.

I remember also with pleasure, the family of Mr. S—, the English Consul at Brussa, in whose house we dined, in company with his daughter and son-in-law, the Consul of Bucharest. That evening, while we talked in the drawing-room of Turner and Landseer, Ruskin and Tennyson, I would almost think myself in a London drawing-room. But at that moment I turned round to the open window, and saw the stars shining with Eastern splendour, and then I remembered where I was.

I was quite sad when I took leave of M. and Mme. S— and their daughters; but sorrows and joys pass quickly on a journey. When I had mounted Mme. S——'s charming little horse she kindly lent me, and was cantering along on our way to Gimlek, where we were to find a boat to take us back to Constantinople, I felt all my spirits return. We accomplished that journey, which usually takes six hours, in four, although we rested twice, at a little kind of caravansery, and had coffee.

Soon after our return from Brussa we left Constantinople, and, if that only is well which ends well, Constantinople was not well, for going on board the French steamer, which was to take us to Messina, was even less agreeable than our embarkation at Rettimo had been. I wished to make a few trifling purchases on my way down to the embarcadair, and my husband therefore proposed to take our luggage to the custom-house, and see it safely on board, while I should join him under the escort of the dragoman. When I got into the boat I much regretted having quitted my husband, for the day being windy and squally, I found the sea very rough. The steamboat was far out, and the waves so high, that the spray quite wetted me, and I had not the warm hand of my husband, but only the cold wet board of the boat to cling to. I was frightened. Still this was nothing to the terror

I felt, when at last safely on board the vessel I found that the luggage had arrived, but not my hubsand.

When he saw that the sea was rough, and knowing that I am of a timid disposition, he had sent on the luggage, thinking he would try to find me and take me on board himself. When I heard this I was nearly in despair, however ridiculous this may seem now. There was I in the steamboat, and my husband still on shore. With the strong current and sea, the boat took much longer time than usual. Might the steamboat not take me to Messina and leave him behind? Would he not, when he found I was gone, take one of those nutshells of a Kaik instead of another boat, and be drowned? for the Kaiks are very dangerous in rough weather. He soon arrived, however, safely in a boat, and I, immensely relieved, but cold and wet and shivering, went down into my cabin to change my wet things. While there I felt the machine begin to work and the boat slowly moving. I hastened on deck. We were just turning round the Seraglio Point, and even under the cold threatening sky that hung over the town, it was a glorious sight. But I turned away from it without regret. It had interested, but not attracted me.

I did not wish for a palace on the Bosphorus, as I had wished for a castle on the Rhine, or a villa on the Bay of Naples. Indeed, I think I would rather live in a little cottage in an English village, than inhabit one of the dreary palaces of Stamboul.

CHAPTER IV.

FROM CONSTANTINOPLE TO FLORENCE.

"Land of the Sun! where'er my footsteps roam,
  My thoughts return to thee—thou art my
    spirit's home."
J. H. PRINGLE.

AND thus the days of Constantinople had gone by, and we were on our voyage back, westward ho! The ship had spread its sails, and the fresh north wind sped us on our way. The sea was very rough; but the movement of the ship, going with the wind, was not unpleasant.

The second night of our voyage I slept very soundly; the waves had rocked me to sleep. Suddenly I was roused by cannon shots, which appeared to be fired-off close to my cabin-window, and shook our vessel. I rose quickly, and found that we had cast anchor in the harbour of Piræus, which was full of men-of-war and other vessels belonging to different nations. All had hoisted their flags, and the Greek vessels were cannonading, for it was the 5th of May—King George's birthday. But I had no time to lose in looking at what was going on in the harbour of Piræus, for in a few hours our boat would leave for Messina, and I wanted to see Athens during that time. I am almost ashamed to say that we did not stop a few days at Athens, but there is only one boat in the week that leaves Athens for Messina, and as we could not spare a week, we had to content ourselves with a few hours. But shall I say the pleasure was not great because it was short? Are not most of the greatest joys of life counted by minutes and hours rather than by weeks and months?

It was a splendid morning, full of clouds and sunshine. The clouds hung over the mountains, but over head smiled the blue Ionian sky. What a pleasant drive it was from Piræus to the Acropolis. After the roads of Turkey it was a great pleasure to drive at a quick pace over a good one. The road was white and dusty, a true summer-road, of which I am very fond. I should most probably have liked it better, if the dust had not been blown into our faces, but I was that morning not in a humour to find fault with anything. I think, in spite of much that is attractive and interesting, I was inwardly glad to be out of Turkey, and if ever I see it again it will not be from choice. The road, after we had driven through some waste and barren land, led through cornfields, where the corn seemed almost ripe; through hayfields and vineyards, which were studded with olive and fruit trees.

Before I left England, the wife of a soldier, who had accompanied her husband to the Crimean war, told me that she had also been at Athens, and that it was "not far from Greece." I found it, however, farther from Piræus than I expected. It is an hour's sharp drive, and although the hour passed pleasantly, it seemed long; perhaps because my wish to see the Acropolis was great. We stopped, however, first before the Temple of Theseus; I had seen it at some distance from the window of our carriage, and had admired the grand and noble structure. When I saw it near I found it was but small, and admired the art that could make a comparatively small and very simple building look so imposing.

A short walk brought us to the Acropolis, and when the keeper unlocked the wooden gate, my heart beat at the thought that I was in ancient Greece. With a strangely solemn feeling I ascended the steps of the Propylæa, and then I found myself surrounded by the glorious remains of those noble works of art which, for simple grandeur and beauty, are unsurpassed by anything the genius of man has since produced. Through those noble columns I beheld the very same features of land and sky on which the sages, the orators, the artists of Greece had gazed. I gathered a handful of flowers that grew among the ruins. I picked up some tiny fragment of marble, and looked at it with a feeling akin to that with which a devout Roman Catholic contemplates a relic of his patron saint. At the same moment my foot stumbled against a broken piece of a cannon-ball. And then I remembered that the "barbarous Turk," more than the ravages of time, had changed these precious monuments of ancient art into ruins; that the Turks had made a powder magazine of the Parthenon, which exploded through a Venetian bomb, and destroyed the Temple of Minerva. And I felt that the Greeks were not to blame for hating them. I felt as if I should have liked to pull down with my own hands the rude, ugly remains of the walls with which they have disfigured the temples of the gods. I felt also very indignant against the Venetians who had no small share in the destruction of those art treasures. They should have known better than to commit such sacrilege. And shall I not say that Lord Elgin, too, committed a great wrong in carrying off those marbles that still adorned the Parthenon? There, under the blue sky of Greece, was their home, and they ought to have remained there. It is true enough that now they can be seen by " the million " that visit the dim rooms of the British Museum; but he has for ever robbed those that might have seen them where they were first placed, of one of the greatest enjoyments art can give to those that love the beautiful.

When we left the fine harbour of Piræus, the Captain pointed out to us the Bay of Salamis, the Throne of Xerxes, the Tomb of Themistocles, and other famous and interesting spots; but I listened only with half attention, for my eyes tried still to distinguish the Acropolis, and I cast many a "long, lingring look behind;" steam and wind, however, carried me quickly away, and soon I saw nothing but the bare, cheerless coast of Greece.

Towards evening the movement of the ship became more violent; the sea rolled in large foaming waves, and when towards nine o'clock we turned Cape St. Angelo, we had some very heavy gusts of wind, which produced such rolling of the boat, that I held to the bench in order to keep my seat. It was a grand sight, but I have no liking for that kind of grandeur, so I stumbled down stairs as well as I could, in order to see no more of it.

On awaking next morning, I found, to my great satisfaction, that the ship moved along with a motion hardly perceptible, the sky was almost cloudless, and the air mild and balmy. That day passed pleasantly. I wrote my letter to my children, read a Waverley Novel, and watched the poor little swallows and turtledoves, that came with weary wing to rest on the masts of our ship. One was so tired that a boy belonging to the crew caught the little wanderer in his hand. We gave it some food and water and a free passage to Sicily, where it was set free.

I awoke early next morning, and peeping through my cabin window, saw in the rays of the rising sun the coast of Calabria. "Ah mio Lindoro presto vedremo l'Italia." I sang, and awoke my husband. We were soon on deck. The sea was calm, and the air as soft and balmy as the day before. The coast of Calabria lay before us, and a little towards the left towered Mount Etna, from whose snow-covered crater arose a white column of smoke, as if Nature was bringing there her morning sacrifice. As we neared the coast the sea became enlivened with boats, whose white sails were reflected in the mirror of the calm sea. We gradually came so close to the coast of Calabria, that we could distinguish houses, trees, gardens, and even human beings and cattle. Through my opera glass I distinguished the very colours of the gaily dressed peasant women that were going to mass, for it was Sunday, and about church time.

The first place at which I looked with special interest was Milito, the little village where Garibaldi ran his ship ashore, when he came to conquer Naples, and was pursued by Neapolitan men-of-war. The Captain that pointed the place out to us, told us that there were still some débris left of the vessel that brought the deliverer of Southern Italy to the shores of Calabria. Then came Reggio, the Neapolitan fortress which the brave Garibaldians took under the command of our friend Colonel Chiassi, and a little further on lay Aspramonte. What a story those three places tell! I looked with a feeling of deep sadness at the mountains over which the flying Garibaldians had carried their wounded General, and thought of Columbus brought back to Spain in chains, of poor John Huss burned at the stake, of Galileo languishing in the prisons of the Inquisition, and how the world has ever cried " crucify him" against its benefactors.

The coast of Calabria looked cheerful and well cultivated ; the mountains have wild strange shapes, but at their feet are orange groves, and mulberry plantations, with here and there, growing in the midst of the bright green, the sombre foliage of the olive. I observed many new comfortable looking houses, with large windows and green shutters, which I hope speak of an improved state of the country, and which contrast favourably with the old dwellings of the Italian peasantry. The latter are generally very wretched looking places, with small dismal looking holes instead of windows.

We stayed a day at Messina, and profited by it to look at the town, the churches, etc. How everything is relative in this world. Had I gone to Messina after visiting Florence and Naples, instead of before, I should most likely have thought it a very insignificant looking place. But after Constantinople and Smyrna, it looked a town of palaces. The nice pavement, the fine large stone houses, with their balconies before every window, on which dark girls in gay Sunday dress stood among flowers.

It looked quite grand, and very pleasant. The churches are rich in precious marbles and gildings, but built in a very degenerate style of architecture. The pictures with which they are decorated generally represent tortured saints, and are even less satisfactory than the buildings themselves. I wanted to see a little of the country, and we therefore took a drive. I saw however nothing of it, except a dusty road between high walls, which seemed to enclose orchards, for the branches of orange, fig, mulberry, and olive trees, were visible above the walls. I cannot tell whether all the roads around Messina are like this one, or if our coachman was to blame for his choice. We found it difficult to understand the Sicilian dialect, and almost required an interpreter to translate it into Italian.

We left Messina the following afternoon. The weather was still calm and beautiful; the sky cloudless, and the sea shining in the sunlight, as calm as a lake. A short time after we had left Messina, we passed Scylla and Charybdis, the first only discernible by a very slight movement in the water, the latter a rather prominent rock on the opposite coast. It must have been very different in the time of Homer, I should think, for even the boldest imagination could not see in the present Scylla and Charybdis, anything like what Homer describes it to have been. As for Schiller's beautiful description of it, in his ballad "The Diver," it is purely imaginative, for Schiller never visited Italy. The next day we passed Stromboli, an island formed by a large volcano rising out of the sea. The mountain, a grand and imposing cone, was in a somewhat active state, much more so than Etna. I was sorry we did not see it by night, for the thick column of smoke that rises out of it, then looks red and fiery. It was however out of sight long before evening, but there were other lights burning through the balmy night, and throwing rays of silver light across the placid waters, Hesperus and " Cynthia's shining orb." It was past midnight before we went down stairs, and we had slept but few hours, when the bustle and noise that always follow the arrival of the boat in port, awoke me. When I got on deck, the sun was rising over Naples. I saw the Bay, and Vesuvius and Capri. All these wonderful names were no longer empty sounds, but had become a reality, and I rejoiced in that thought.

I have not spoken of any of my travelling companions since I left Constantinople. The reason is, that they hardly deserved any special notice. They were such people as any one is likely to meet. Several English families, that had wintered abroad, and returned most of them with coughs and sore throats. Some of the girls were very pretty, perhaps all the more so because they looked so fragile, it seemed one cold East wind would blow the pretty blossoms away. Then there was a rich Jewess from Constantinople, with three daughters, who were all " musical young ladies." They were going to some European watering-place, not for their health though, I should think, for they looked as strong and hearty as one could wish. The Messageries Impériales steamers are unfortunately provided with a piano, which I consider a most inconsiderate arrangement on the part of the Company; for I had to listen for several hours daily to the performances of these young ladies, playing either singly or in couples. The nuisance became almost intolerable, when they were joined at Messina by a musical young gentleman, an officer from Malta, who, between the fantasias and sonatas of the young ladies, treated us to a succession of quadrilles and polkas. It broke into and spoiled the calm enjoyment of one of the most beautiful moonlight-nights on the Mediterranean, when nature seemed so hushed and still, that I involuntarily spoke in whispers.

There were also two interesting honey-moon couples on board: one of them always sitting in out-of-the-way corners, so that perhaps I might have been altogether unaware of their presence, so little were they in any body's way, had they not turned up regularly at meal times. The other couple never turned up at all, at least not the lady. She was very poorly, and in fair or foul weather always lying down in the Ladies' Saloon; to the open door of which the devoted young husband came ever so many times a day, offering lemonade, coffee, and other refreshments to the sufferer, who however seemed unable to relish any thing.

And I must not forget Miss L—, because of the singular adventure that happened to her. She was of middle age and rather delicate constitution, had spent the winter with some friends at Malta, and was now on her way home. We had been neighbours at dinner, and exchanged a few words. Early in the evening, after we had left Messina, where she came on board, she came to me in great agitation, and asked my advice under what were certainly trying circumstances. The stewardess in showing her to her cabin, had said that there would be but one other occupant, viz. a "jeune demoiselle." How surprised and horrified therefore was the poor lady when, wishing to retire early, she had gone into her cabin, and saw standing before the other berth a pair of man's boots, and a man lying dressed on it, who had his face covered with a silk handkerchief. She rushed back and told the stewardess that there was a man in her cabin. The stewardess however replied good humouredly, and with a smiling face: "Non, Madame, ce n'est pas un homme, mais une jeune demoiselle noire qui s'habille comme çà." She told her at the same time that she was sorry there was no empty berth in any other cabin, as she seemed to dislike sleeping with the "jeune demoiselle noire." At this information, the slight knowledge of the French language which Miss L— possessed, seemed quite to forsake her, she found no words to reply, and came in despair to me, as the only person with whom she had exchanged a few words on board. "What am I to do?" so the poor thing concluded her story, "I cannot sleep in the Saloon because it is full of gentlemen, and to remain on deck would be sure to make me ill, as I am very susceptible to colds." I took her to my husband, as the tribunal to which I appeal in difficult cases, and he at once reassured her by his promise that he would take care she should not sleep in the same room with the black person, who travelled under the name of a "jeune demoiselle." He went straight to the Captain, and what the stewardess said she could not do, the Captain arranged. She slept comfortably in the same room with some other ladies, who neither wore male attire, nor "the shadowy livery of a warmer sun."

Her gratitude to my husband was boundless, and she remained my constant companion till we reached Naples, where we landed, while she proceeded to Genoa and Marseilles. We saw the "jeune demoiselle," as we called the black person, a good deal on deck and at meals. Miss L— always kept as far as possible away from her, and I did not wonder at it. In looking at the African I felt more than ever, that, although in theory the Americans may be to blame for their manifest dislike to the Negroes; in practice I should find it very difficult not to do as they do, and avoid any intercourse with them. And I admired more than ever the heavenly kindness of Mrs. Beecher Stow's little Eva, who broke her heart at the fate of this race. I forget at this moment, if, according to Mr. Darwin's theory, we have a common origin with them, or are descended from them. In the latter case I hope nobody will ever ask me the question Farinato addresses to Dante in the Inferno: "Chi fur i maggior tuoi" — as I should be rather ashamed to mention these ancestors.

Goethe quotes Pliny's description of Naples, and what Goethe did I surely may be allowed to do. Instead, therefore, of trying to describe Naples myself, I will translate what he has quoted: "So happy, lovely, blessed is that region, that one perceives Nature has rejoiced in her work there. Such vital air, such continued salutary clemency of the sky, such fruitful fields, such sunny hills, such innoxious woods, such shady groves, such useful forests, such airy mountains, such far-extending cornfields, such an abundance of vines and olive-trees, such fine wool of the sheep, such fat necks of the oxen, so many lakes, such an abundance of irrigating rivers and streams, so many seas, so many harbours! The earth opens her bosom everywhere to commerce, and, almost anxious to assist man, stretches her arms into the sea." After reading such a description, the well-known "Vedi Napoli e poi mori," does not seem very exaggerated; nor when Goethe writes of his father: "It is said that he who has seen a ghost can never more be joyful, so on the contrary one might have said of him (his father) that he could never become quite unhappy, because he thought himself always back again at Naples." That the days I spent there brought me enjoyment and delight, every one will easily suppose. People always call Paris a "gay" place, and such no doubt it is, still thousands and thousands lead a dreary and dismal life there, which seems hardly possible in Naples. Nature supplies all the necessaries of life in such abundance that even poverty ceases to cause real suffering. The climate is so mild that the want of what we should call indispensable clothing brings no discomfort; while a plate of macaroni, a dried fish, or a slice of melon seems to be all the food they require. They are exceedingly fond of music and dancing, and the Neapolitan airs are lively and pretty, and pleased me more than any I have heard in Italy. The performers who sing before the hotel, the caffés and restaurants, and accompany their songs with the guitar and the liveliest expression and gesticulations, look delightfully merry and cunning. Many of them improvise in a ready, pretty manner. Who can be sad and morose in a place like this, where everybody looks smiling, good-natured and contented? To be merry, joyful and happy lies in the air there, and is contagious like an epidemic. And I do not think the expression of good-nature and contentment one sees in almost every face, belies their feelings. The Neapolitans appeared to be very kind-hearted, and to delight in giving pleasure. We received, during our short stay at Naples, several marks of good will from them, of which I remember one especially with pleasure. We had stopped, on our way back from a short excursion to Posilipo, at a pretty restaurant, where we took some refreshments on an open platform overlooking the sea. While sitting there, and looking at the Bay and all the beauty surrounding it, a boat passed with a merry party in it, four of whom were amateur musicians. They played on two guitars, a flute, and a trombone. As soon as they saw us they stopped the boat right under our platform and played a pretty Neapolitan air, with the simple intention of giving us pleasure. When they had finished they greeted us and left. We returned the kind salute, and listened to their " renewed strain " till it became indistinct, and the accompanying sounds of the trombone only reached us.

After the great variety of Eastern costume the dress of the Neapolitans looked rather tame. The dress of the women is neat and clean, their full black hair is well plaited and shines like satin; but they wear nothing that can be called a costume, and I found even crinoline introduced to a great extent. If it were not for the dress of the different orders of monks and nuns, of boatmen and fishermen, and here and there a contadina in her pretty dress, the crowd would be not much more picturesque than an English one, from which however it would be easily distinguished by the darker complexion of the people, the animated features, and the lively gesticulations with which they accompany all they say.

We were at Naples the week after the first Sunday in May, which is one continual festival in honour of St. Gennaro, the great patron saint of Naples. Thus I had an opportunity of witnessing the celebrated miracle of liquefaction of the blood of the saint, which is kept in two phials in the chapel " del Tesoro " adjoining the cathedral, for the blood liquefies daily during the festival when high mass is celebrated. The chapel is wonderfully magnificent; the three altars with their ornaments, and the statues of more than forty saints, being all of silver. The most magnificent of all is, of course, that of Saint Gennaro standing on the high altar, whose mitre of gold is covered with precious stones of great size, and who wears round his neck enough ornaments to deck a whole crowd of queens and duchesses. They are the gifts of different kings and queens of Naples. Napoleon I., who stripped so many churches of their treasures, made a present to this all-powerful saint, and Victor Emanuel seems to have thought that in this respect he too must follow the example of his predecessors, for the saint wears two magnificent crosses of amethysts and diamonds, the gift of the Rè Galantuomo. My husband did not approve of this, and even expressed a wish that Garibaldi had melted down the gold and silver saints, and invested the money so obtained in schools for the people, and other public and charitable institutions.

But who can tell if even Garibaldi, the idol of the people of Naples, and the saint they perhaps most adore after St. Gennaro, could have done this. The priest to whom I expressed my astonishment, that the treasures of this chapel had escaped the vicissitudes of so many revolutions and wars, said it was evidently a miracle wrought by the saint.

If the great St. Gennaro has as yet escaped peculation, the common little saints that used to stand at every street corner of Naples, have not fared so well of late. They were all of them removed in one night, by order of General La Marmora, then Governor of Naples. The people, especially the women, became clamorous and noisy on the discovery next morning, but were told that the Governor was so fond of the Saints, that he wished to take better care of them. He had therefore removed the Saints from their uncomfortable quarters in the street, to snugger ones in the Churches and Convents, where they would be much better off. This entirely satisfied the crowd.

The removal of the Saints, and that of the pigs of St. Antonio, which Garibaldi effected, has much changed the appearance of the streets of Naples. The pigs of the Convent of St. Antonio, that used to run about in the principal streets of Naples, even in the fine Strada Toledo, and which lived upon public charity, were a terrible nuisance. The ignorant populace held these pigs of the holy fathers in great veneration, and fed them well, and I have been assured on good authority, that if a man had with his cart or carriage run over a child in the streets, he might possibly have escaped unpunished, but had he hurt a pig in that way, the infuriated mob would almost have killed him.

The morning I went to hear High Mass in the Chapel del Tesoro, it presented an animated and magnificent spectacle. The windows were darkened by crimson blinds, to keep the strong sunlight out, and the chapel was lighted up by numberless candles, the light of which was reflected by the silver ornaments that deck the whole chapel. The way up to the altar was lined with soldiers, I suppose to prevent disturbances in the eager crowd that longed to kiss the liquefied blood.

The people walked up in good order to the altar, but on the sides down which they returned, there was a good deal of squeezing and pushing. The priest that held the little glass case, containing the two phials in his hand, and who showed them to the congregation, shook the liquefied blood about, and thrust the case into the people's faces with so rudely irreverent a manner, that I, who am no believer in the miracle, felt shocked; what impression it made upon the other people I cannot tell. They looked however quite contented and pleased. They were mostly priests and nuns, and persons of the lower orders, but I observed also some who appeared to belong to the upper classes.

While the crowd kissed the blood of the Saint the choir sang a most beautiful mass, and the rich voices with which bountiful Nature has endowed so many of her children under the blue sky of Naples, filled the chapel with harmony, and made the chords of my heart vibrate in unison. There was a bass voice among them that reminded me of Lablache.

On the evening of the same day I had witnessed the miracle of the liquefaction in the Chapel del Tesoro, the son of the famous conjuror Bosco repeated the trick before the boxes crowded with elegant ladies at the Theatre St. Carlo, but I did not go to see it. Ever since I am out of my teens, I no longer care for conjuring tricks; besides I had seen it done so well in the morning. I was however told that the trick in the evening succeeded quite as well, and was repeated several times before a smiling and applauding audience. I visited most of the other principal churches of Naples. The Church of St. Severo, is full of fine modern statues. One representing a man who is trying to free himself from the meshes of a net in which he is entangled, and which is called " the snares of the world," is very clever. Another one called " Modesty" is graceful, but as a representation of modesty, might have a somewhat thicker veil. At the Museo Borbonico, now called " Reale," I admired some of the finest Greek marbles I have ever seen. The grand Torro Farnese, the wonderful Hercules, of the same famous collection, a Flora, that looks something between a Juno and a Venus, stately and graceful at the same time, the most charming representation of virgin youth I have ever seen. There is a whole room full of Venuses, of which one is certainly very beautiful, although apparently too conscious of her charms to please me very much.

"I must go up Mount Vesuvius before we leave Naples," I said to my husband, and he, not less desirous than myself to visit a volcano, set out with me early the next morning, for the ascent of the mountain.

I know it is considered a beautiful sight to see the sun rise from the top of Vesuvius, but as it rises in the middle of May at a most unreasonably early hour, we despaired of getting to the top before the sun, so we let the god travel alone for several hours, and did not leave our hotel in the Chiatamone till a little after six o'clock. An hour's quick drive brought us to Resina. Our way to the latter led us through the village of St. Giovanni, where one sees nothing but macaroni and pigs. Most of the houses are small macaroni manufactories, and the fresh macaroni are on long sticks, hung out into the street to dry. Most of the manufacturers keep a pig, which is tied to some post in the street, not far from the door of the house, or if a very tame, good little pig, runs about free.

After St. Giovanni, we passed through Portici,

the home of Masaniello and his poor sister Fenella. Here there are delightful villas, with gardens sloping down to the bay, and close to it lies Resina, where the ascent of the mountain on horseback begins. There used to be a fine carriage road as far as St. Salvator, which is about an hour's ride up the mountain, but the lava streams of the great eruption of 1859, have entirely destroyed it. We had not been more than ten minutes on our horses, when we came to these formidable traces of the last great eruption of the volcano. In broad thick masses the lava had flowed down the sides of the mountain into the blooming orchards and fruitful vineyards, to which the dark, dead rivers of stone presented a striking contrast.

These lava streams have a strange and diverse appearance. Sometimes the surface is roughly even and resembles immense masses of curiously twisted burnt trunks, and branches of trees. At other places it is more like a roughly ploughed field that by a sharp frost has become still more broken up than by the plough. Between the lava are large beds of ashes and cinders.

The ride to the foot of the cone, which lasted about an hour and a half, presented no difficulty, for the road rises very gradually and is broad, and lava presents a rough surface on which the horses' feet do not slip. The cone must be climbed on foot, and is a very tiring piece of work even with the assistance of two guides, the one to pull you up with the help of a band fastened round his waist, the other pushing you up by placing one of his hands against your back. As climbing does not easily tire me I wanted to walk up, to which my husband however objected; so I had to sit down in a chair in which the guides carried me up. One guide in front held the two poles which were fastened to the chair in his hands, two men behind carried each one on his shoulder, and thus kept the chair in a horizontal position. It must be very hard work indeed to carry any body for an hour up so steep an ascent; for my husband, although he was assisted in the already described manner by two guides, found it very tiring indeed. The men did it however cheerfully, and with less appearance of fatigue than I had expected. When we had reached the top, and my husband and the men had rested awhile, we walked to the brink of the crater, and now I saw, with my own eyes, the strange and grand spectacle to the description of which I remember to have listened with almost incredulous wonder when a little school girl, and which to see I had longed for ever since we had passed Mount Etna and Stromboli.

The volcano was in a very fair state of activity. Thick volumes of smoke issued from it, and about every two minutes there was a loud report as of thunder or cannon, and then flames appeared, and ashes and stones were ejected flying high up into the air, and falling down with a rattling noise. It must not however be thought that we stood close to the terrible opening out of which rose the flames and smoke. Within the large crater from the brink of which we witnessed the spectacle, rises, what looks a Vesuvius on a smaller scale, and on the top of this, which is however below the level of the place where we stood, is the real crater. It is very fascinating to watch the eruptions, and we found it difficult to turn our backs upon it, and look a little at the scene around us in the beautiful world below.

The top of Vesuvius looks terribly dreary; the dread abode of horror and destruction. Nothing but the dark lava stones and ashes all around. There is of course no trace of animal or vegetable life visible anywhere. The sad monotony is however a little relieved by the different colours of the lava and the stones; especially by the bright yellow of the sulphur one sees in large quantities.

This hideous image of death and destruction rises abruptly out of Elysian plains and vallies; its foot is washed by the azure sea dotted with emerald islands, and above smiles a limpid sky.

The view is very extensive, because Vesuvius is a mountain of considerable altitude; yet as it rises so abruptly out of the plain and sea, the view has the distinctness of no great distance, which adds much to its charm. It is lovely on all sides; but from the point that overlooks Naples, the Bay and its lovely shores, the Mediterranean, and the islands of Capri, Ischia and Procida, it is deservedly considered one of the most lovely in the world.

In going up the volcano the guides had chosen a stony, rough stream of lava, which affords a safe footing; in going down, on the contrary, they chose a bed of fine cinders and ashes, and ran or slid rapidly down. What it had taken us an hour to ascend, my husband descended in six minutes, and I, chair and all, took only about double that time. It is a very dusty affair, the black ashes whirl up under the feet of the men, and envelope one completely. Never was a tepid bath more refreshing than the one I enjoyed in the evening after I had come home from my visit to Vesuvius.

The guides had pointed out to us the lava streams of the different eruptions, and the immense stones and pieces of rock which were ejected by the volcano in 1822. In looking at these formidable pieces of rock, of which some were at a great distance from the crater, one gets an idea of the power that is working within it, and the fate of Herculaneum and Pompeii becomes intelligible. The latter place we had visited the day before. All I felt there is expressed in those few words: " Sic transit gloria mundi." But never before had I realized so fully what the instability of all earthly greatness means. In this city of the dead I felt far, far removed from the present, and my mind for a moment seemed to realize what the future really means. A time, when the lovely city I had just left would have disappeared from the face of the earth, and its old site be a matter of doubt and uncertainty, when the language of Dante would survive perhaps in his book only, when the very features of sea and mountain around me might be changed; for had not eighteen hundred years ago, the waves of the gulf washed the walls of Pompeii that now lies far inland, and another Vesuvius burned than the one we ascended? And I saw with my mind's eye the proud city across the sea, which I had left a few months before, as Macaulay, thinking of a time to come, describes it, a heap of ruins; and a traveller in a strange dress, speaking a language which is not yet formed, sitting on a broken arch of London Bridge, meditating like me at that moment on the truth of the words, " Sic transit gloria mundi." We did not, as Murray recommends, enter Pompeii by the Strada dei Sepolcri, but through the Porta del Mare, and I liked it better, as the Strada de Sepolcri forms the fittest finale of the town.

I have heard of people who have been disappointed in Pompeii, others have said the same of the Acropolis. I cannot understand such people. They must be more dead than the very stones there, for they spoke to me, and what they said moved me deeply. When I first entered the city of the dead, I felt strange and bewildered like in a dream. Surely "reality is stranger than fiction." What can be more strange than that the sun should shine again into the streets, and light up the painted walls and mosaic pavement of Pompeii. And yet so it is. That very old Pompeii, that lay for nearly eighteen centuries buried, is risen again. We walk through its streets, and tread the very stones worn out by the footsteps of Roman citizens, and by the wheels of their chariots.

We see their houses, their temples, their judgment halls, their baths and theatres, their gardens and court-yards, in which however the little fountain is silenced for ever. In walking into their houses we seem to become strangely familiar with their former inhabitants; we see everywhere traces of their being, of their virtues and vices, of their greatness and their folly. I daresay by night the spirits of the departed haunt the silent town; but it was by broad cheerful daylight that I visited it, and therefore it seemed inhabited only by pretty little lizards, which I saw flitting about on every wall, and between the delicate ferns that grow in the silent streets of Pompeii.

Of our journey from Naples to Leghorn, there is not much to be said, although it was very pleasant. We went with the Italian steamer "Principe Umberto," which was filled with passengers, most of whom were going like ourselves to Florence, for the Dante festival, which was to be celebrated there on the 14th, 15th, and 16th of May. Several of the passengers were deputies sent to Florence from different towns in Calabria. The company was lively and merry. The piano in the saloon sounded almost the whole day, but being touched by skilful fingers it did not annoy me like the performances of the young ladies from Constantinople, or the quadrilles of the young English officer.

We arrived at Leghorn on the 13th of May,

after a journey of twenty-four hours, there we remained the night, not daring to proceed to Florence, for we knew that all the hotels were over-crowded, and that we should find it difficult to get a room if we arrived late at night.

After a stroll through the town, which is a well built modern place, we went to rest, in order to be better able to bear the fatigues, and enjoy the pleasures of the days to come.

CHAPTER V.

THE DANTE FESTIVAL AT FLORENCE.

" Del bel paese la dove il si suona."

DANTE.

AND now the great day had come, the 14th of May, 1865! I had to rise very early, for we intended to leave by the first train, which started from Leghorn at four o'clock in the morning. Although rather averse to early rising in England, it cost me no effort here. The thought of going to Florence roused me, besides the warm bright twilight of an Italian May morning lighted up my bedroom, and the street was already full of people, all in holiday dress, and taking the road towards the station, in order to secure places in the train that was to take them to Florence.

We were not the last in the crowd, and three hours after, arrived at Florence, where Italy was going to celebrate on that day the sixth centenary anniversary of the birth of Dante. Truly this solemn event happened " in the fulness of time," and every thing concurred to make it as splendid and happy a festival as any nation has ever celebrated. Now, for the first time, the grand idea of Dante, a free and united Italy, has almost become a complete reality, and the hearts of all his people rejoice that from the Alps to Mount Etna, one law now reigns, and hopefully trust that the other great thought of Dante, the deliverance of the Church from the burden of temporal power, will ere long also become a reality. The disappointment and irritation the Italians felt at the loss of Savoy and Nice, has almost entirely passed, while what they have gained has still all the charm of a new possession, and something of the passion and enthusiasm of honeymoon-love in it. Is it therefore to be wondered at that the people of Italy rejoiced on the 14th of May? that every countenance wore a smile, and that their lively eyes sparkled with joy!

The festival happening in Spring-time was also a favourable circumstance. Dante, near the entrance of Hell, felt comforted because it was "la bella stagione," was it therefore not natural that it added much to the splendour and enjoyment of a fête in " blooming Florence !" Had the anniversary happened in December or January, where could the flowers have come from, and the glory of the golden sunshine round Dante's statue. A pelting rain might easily have damped the enthusiasm of his countrymen, as it would most certainly have spoiled the pretty bonnets of his fair compatriots, that made so nice a show in seats round the Piazza Santa Croce.

Most favourable for the celebration of the anniversary of Dante's birth, was lastly, that it happened at Florence, the very town in all the world best adapted for the celebration of such an event.

Fancy a national festival at Paris or London! The size of those towns does not admit of a general decoration; but even if such a miracle could be performed, nobody would ever see a tenth part of it, as one would be nearly dead with fatigue getting half way from the Marble Arch to St. Paul's. Another serious drawback are the immense multitudes that inhabit these monster towns, and create unpleasant crowds, which, to all that have not nerves of iron, and great physical strength, destroy all feeling of enjoyment. None of these unfavourable conditions existed in Florence. It is but a little place, though such a gem of a town, and can therefore be uniformly decorated, changed into a gigantic palace, through whose halls and corridors the inhabitants and visitors, that do not number by millions, gaily move. And such a place Florence appeared on that day. All the houses had red, green, or yellow silk hangings falling down from their windows, and were besides richly decorated with pictures, busts, flags, flowers, and evergreens. The noble architecture of the town, the nice clean streets, which are neither too narrow to look sombre, nor too broad not to be easily spanned by garlands of flowers, all united to produce the happiest effect. On all the principal places, statues of great Italians had been placed, or trophies in remembrance of some great national event, which happened on that particular spot. There was a great number of them; for the Florentines boast, and not without some reason, that if a stone were to mark every glorious memory of the town, there would hardly be a stone in Florence that did not deserve special distinction. I could not attempt to find out what all the statues and trophies meant, but even if I had looked at them all, and remembered every inscription, I could not enumerate them here, else what is to be but a chapter would become a volume.

I must however mention a fine statue of Galileo, on the Piazza Sante Maria Novella, with the following inscription:—

"A Galileo.
Finirà la tua gloria
quando il genere umano
cessi di vedere il sole ed abitare la terra."*

Near the Ponte alla Carraia, there was a statue to Goldoni, the great writer of comedies, and on the Piazza del Duomo, those of the famous architects Arnolfo and Brunelesco. On the houses where celebrated men were born, lived, or died, tablets were placed recording their names and deeds, ornamented with banners, wreaths of flowers and laurels, and often with the bust or portrait of the illustrious dead.

The Bruneleschi palace, where Michael Angelo lived and died, and which still contains his books, furniture, etc., interested me much. On a house in the Corso, I noticed the following inscription:—

O voi che per la via d'amor passate
volgete uno sguardo alle mure
ove naque nell' aprile del 1266
Beatrice Portinari,
prima e purissima fiamma,
che accese il genio
del Divino Poeta
Dante Alighieri.†

---

* Thy glory will end, when the human race shall have ceased to see the sun, and to inhabit the earth.

† You that walk in the path of love, cast a look upon these walls, where in April 1266, was born Beatrice Portinari, etc.

The house of Giovanni Battista Strozzi, named the Blind, the great scholar and philosopher of the 17th century, was beautifully decorated. I remarked also Frescobaldi's, the friend of Dante, which stands in the Via Maggio, and not far from it, on the Piazza Santa Trinità, the house in which Robert Dudley, an English mathematician of the 17th century lived, whose memory still survives in Florence.

In Sta. Maria Maggiore, I observed a tablet which marks the spot where Brunetto Latini, Dante's master, is buried. Under the name was written the following line from the Divina Comedia, which is deservedly considered a grander and more lasting monument than any that could be erected in marble:

" M'insegnavate come l'uom s'eterna."*

On the Piazza del Duomo, is the " Sasso di Dante," a stone upon which the great man often sat in meditations, as lofty and grand as the glorious Dome on which he was silently gazing.

In a niche in the wall over that spot, was placed the bust of Dante, surrounded by laurel wreaths and flowers. The Piazza dei Signori, looked magnificent and most beautiful of all that part

* You taught me how a man becomes immortal.

which is formed by the Loggia dei Lanzi, under whose noble arches are placed some of the finest works of art: the Theseus by Benvenuto Cellini, the Rape of the Sabines by Giovanni di Bologna, and others. This gem of architecture is at all times splendid, but now its walls were covered with the most exquisite Gobelin tapestry, after designs by Michael Angelo. They represented the history of Adam and Eve, from their creation to their expulsion from Paradise.

The greatest care had however been bestowed on the decoration of the Piazza Santa Croce, where the inauguration of the national monument to Dante was to take place. This piazza is a large oblong space, whose houses were covered with flowers and rich red silk hangings, and the background was formed by the splendid marble façade of the church of Santa Croce. The piazza had been boarded and carpeted all over, and raised seats were erected for the spectators who had obtained tickets. When these seats and the windows round the piazza were all filled, principally with ladies, in the most elegant spring toilets, the effect was the gayest imaginable.

Behind the seats were placed thirty-eight paintings imitating bas-relief, illustrating the life of Dante. The first represented him when, nine years old, he first saw Beatrice, in the house of her father; the last showed his burial in Ravenna. There were also the portraits of about forty celebrated contemporaries, translators, or commentators of Dante.

Round the piazza were placed rich banners of Florence and Tuscany, the poles of which were festooned with wreaths of laurels and flowers. On the pole of each banner was placed a tablet with some verses from the great poem of Dante; many of which anticipated the great political and religious events of the day, for the accomplishment of which 550 years ago, Dante had longed with passionate desire. I noted down a few, which I will transcribe here.

> Soleva Roma, che'l buon mondo feo,
> Duo Soli aver, che l'una e l'altra strada
> Faccan vedere, e del mondo e di Deo.
> L'un l'altro ha spento, ed è giunta la spada
> Col pastorale: e l'un coll 'altro insieme
> Per viva forza mal convien che vada.*
>
> Purgatorio, Canto 26.

---

* Rome, that turned once the world to good
Was wont to boast two suns, whose several beams
Cast light in either way; the world's and God's.
One since has quenched the other, and the sword
Is grafted on the crook; and so conjoined
Each must perforce decline to worse, unawed
By fear of other. *Cary's translation.*

Di oggimai, che la chiesa di Roma
Per confondere in sè duo reggimenti
Cade nel fango, e sè brutta e la soma.*
      Purg. Canto 26.
Ahi, Costantin, di quanto mal fu matre
Non la tua conversion, ma quella dote,
Che da te prese il primo ricco patre!†
      Inferno, Canto 19.
Non fu nostra intenzion, ch'a destra mano
De'nostri successor parte sedesse
Parte dall'altra, del popal cristiano,
Nè che le chiavi, che mi fûr concesse
Divenisser segnacolo in vessillo
Che contra i battezzati combattesse.‡
      Paradiso, Canto 27.

---

* The Church of Rome,
Mixing two governments that ill assort,
Hath missed her footing, fallen into the mire,
And there herself and burden much defiled.

† Ah Constantine! to how much ill gave birth
Not thy conversion, but that plentous dower
Which the first wealthy Father gained from thee.
      Cary's Dante.

‡ No purpose was of ours
That on the right hand of our successors,
Part of the Christian people should be set,
And part upon their left; nor that the keys,
Which were vouchsafed me, should for ensign serve
Unto the banners, that do levy war
On the baptized.

> Lo maggior don, che Dio per sua larghezza
> Fêsse creando, ed alla sua bontate
> Più conformato, e quel ch'ei più apprezza,
> Fu della volontà la libertate
> Di che le creature intelligenti,
> E tutte e sole, furo e son dotate.*
>
> *Paradiso, Cant.* v.

Through the happy crowd that thronged the festive streets of Florence, we wound our way to the Piazza St. Croce, after having rested a little while at the house of a friend, who had kindly invited us to stay with him during the festival, as it was almost impossible to get any good accommodation in the over-crowded hotels.

We arrived at the Piazza soon after ten o'clock, and found a place near to the throne, erected in the centre of the Piazza, on which the King took his seat during the ceremony, I could therefore understand much of what the Gonfaloniere and Father Giuliani said when they addressed him.

We had not waited long, when the ringing of the bells of the Palazzo Vecchio, announced that

---

* Supreme of gifts which God, creating, gave
  Of his free bounty, sign most evident
  Of goodness, and in his account most prized,
  Was liberty of will, the boon wherewith
  All intellectual creatures, and them sole,
  He hath endowed.

the procession had begun, and before long the music of the band was heard. The guards on horseback, who rode in front of the procession, appeared and cleared the way. Then came a band of music, followed by the representatives of the Italian press, who were succeeded by those of the Italian artists, among which were several ladies, the only females who took part in the procession. Foremost among them I noticed Mdme. Ristori, who walked along with the grace and dignity of a queen.

The ladies wore, as a head covering, instead of bonnets, the pretty and becoming black Italian veil. And then came an endless procession of deputations from every town in Italy, occasionally intercepted by bands of music. Each deputation carried a banner, the beauty and elegance of which surpassed anything of the kind I had ever seen.

When the whole procession had arrived, and ranged itself round the Piazza, and more than three hundred silk banners waved and glittered in the sunshine, the sight was magnificent beyond description. The beautiful banners were, after the ceremony, presented by the different deputations to the municipality of Florence, and will be kept as a remembrance of the 14th of May, 1865.

The deputations of the different towns and provinces followed each other in an alphabetical order, with the exception of the municipal bodies of Florence and Ravenna, representing Dante's birth-place, and the town where he died and was buried; these were the last in the procession. The red fleur-de-lis of Florence was loudly cheered, so were the arms of Ravenna, and the same honour was bestowed on the sign of the Wolf suckling twin boys, which was carried by a deputation from Rome. This banner had crape attached to it. The cheers became most enthusiastic when the winged Lion of Venice appeared, also with the sign of mourning, and followed by a long train of exiles from that unhappy place. The generous and easily moved Italians were loud in their expression of sympathy; the men shouted and clapped their hands, the women burst into tears and waved their handkerchiefs.

I noticed also a deputation from Trieste. I am no politician, so I may be mistaken; but I thought Austria had an undeniable right to that province, and therefore looked upon its deputation rather as an intruder. And I must not forget to mention two Dominican Friars, who had come with us from Naples, and were sent from some fraternity there.

The banner they carried bore the inscription "Roma per Capitale," and they received many signs of good-will as they passed in the procession, being the only priests that had taken any part in the festival, or shown any feeling that was not indifference or even hostility to it.

The priesthood of Florence behaved in a most ungracious manner. All the beautiful churches of Florence, which thousands of eager strangers wished to see, were closed, except for a few hours daily when mass was said; and money, which usually opens those doors so readily, was of no avail; so that many who could not stay after the festival was over, saw but few, and those often at great inconvenience, being obliged to profit by the short time of service when they were open.

Soon after the procession had ranged itself round the Piazza, and the bands were playing joyful tunes, loud cheers announced the approach of the King, the first King of Italy, the representative of its unity and liberty! The Rè Galantuomo took his seat opposite the veiled statue, and was, as soon as the cheers had subsided, addressed by the Gonfaloniere, who was, like the rest of the municipal body, dressed in his robes of office, which closely resemble those worn by the magistrates at the time of Dante. The moment he had concluded his speech, the covering dropped, and there stood in the midst of his people, indescribably grand, with an expression both austere and kind, sad and happy, Dante the divine. There was a long pause, then a murmur, then loud cheering. It was a moment never to be forgotten. I looked at the statue again next day, and found some fault with it; it takes too wide a stride, the right arm is thrown too far backwards, but at the moment of uncovering I observed none of those defects; it appeared grand and imposing, and the expression of the face worthy of the great soul that once had animated its features.

But where was at that moment Italy's Hero; he, who had done more than any one living or dead for the realization of the great thought of Dante's life; he, who resembled the great dead more than any living Italian, in his unselfish, undying love of his country, in his pure and blameless life? A solitary exile, on a bare rock of Caprera sat Giuseppe Garibaldi on that joyful day. Close by the side of the King, as when he entered the Cathedral of Naples, there Italy ought to have prepared a seat for him. But he seemed forgotten by every body. No where did I see a bust that portrayed his noble features; I heard no voice raise the cry, " Evviva Garibaldi!"

Thus let it be! But surely the day will come, as came the Dante day of Florence, when Italy will pay her tribute of honour to her Hero, as she did that day to her Poet. Then will multitudes flock together, and men looking at his noble image, will call out with beating hearts, " Behold our deliverer," and women will weep, and lifting up their children will cry, " To him we owe it, that we are Italians." And I missed the presence of another man, of one who, although in another way, laboured as earnestly and successfully for his country. But Camillo Cavour after a life of toil and trouble, rests peacefully at Santena. He saw but the dawn of the bright day that has now arisen over his country. When the king and the people had for some time gazed at the figure that had appeared so suddenly in their midst, Padre Giuliani made a short speech, of which the words " Onorate l'altissimo Poeta, la sua grand anima è placata,"* made a deep impression. Amidst the sounds of a joyful chorus, singing a hymn to Dante, I left the Piazza Santa Croce.

In the coolness of the night, after having rested from the fatigues of the morning, we took an open carriage for a drive through the illuminated town.

---

* Let us honour the sublime Poet, his great soul is appeased.

I had never seen an illumination abroad, and was enchanted. Oh how little do we understand such things in England! I had always thought the blazing gas-stars, crowns, Prince of Wales' feathers, and V. R.'s, stuck against some dark shapeless building, very meaningless and hideous, and for the last ten years nothing could ever persuade me to turn out on an illumination night. It was in Florence I learned that such a spectacle can be imposing and lovely. We commit two glaring faults in our illuminations in England. The first is that we employ gas, instead of oil lamps, which glares and dazzles instead of illuminating ; secondly, instead of lighting up our buildings architecturally, we stick some ornament against them, which is perfectly unmeaning and arbitrary. I wonder that any one who is not a child, can care to look at a thing only because it is bright. The Florentines had illuminated their beautiful town, especially its most imposing buildings, with lamps arranged in a way to bring out every outline in a blaze of light. The stones of the walls appeared transparent, as if the light which was merely reflected by them, proceeded from them. The wonderful structures of the Palazzo Vecchio, the Palazzo della Podestà, the Palazzo Pitti, and of the Duomo, served as a scaffolding for the fairy palaces that burned through the night. And if possible the effect they produced was even surpassed by the illumination of the Lung'Arno, where the long rows of innumerable lights along the banks, and round the arches of the bridges, were reflected in the placid waters of the Arno, in which they formed long lines of golden light, and wonderfully increased the effect of the illumination above. How I wish that we could be treated to a similar sight in London. Why are the noble mansions, for instance the Club-houses in St. James', not lighted up in this way, instead of being actually disfigured by senseless ornaments, which I hear are nevertheless very costly? Will none of the honourable members of those clubs, who have seen and admired an illumination of St. Peter's at Rome, or of the Pitti Palace at Florence, treat the London sightseers to such a spectacle? To hope that such a thing should be done with the houses of Parliament, or St. Paul's, is perhaps too bold a wish.

In the principal squares of the town were stationed bands of music and choirs; and thus a happy crowd that behaved with a gentleness and politeness, which astonished me as much as the illumination, moved along through the cool pleasant night to the sounds of joyful music.

And thus ended the first day of Dante's great festival.

On the second day there was a matinée musicale, where a " Hymn to Beatrice," a chorus called " Dante's return to Florence," and other pieces, were sung, and in the evening there was a grand concert in the Teatro Pagliano, where a " Dante Symphony," the " Ave Maria" of Dante, and other appropriate pieces were executed, but as I was present at neither, I cannot say any thing about them. I spent several hours that day in the Palazzo della Podestà, and examined the " Espositione Dantesca."

Its object was to make us as much as possible acquainted with all that related to Dante and his time. There was a large collection of portraits of Dante, of which an excellent copy of one by Giotto, pleased me most. There were also several pictures of which he was the subject, but they had little intrinsic value. Among the paintings illustrating some part of the Divina Comedia, I noticed but one good picture, a modern one by Benvenuto d'Arezzi. It represents Ugolino and his sons ; it is however, not so good as the one by Reynolds, at Knole House, and which depicts this terrible story almost as powerfully as the twenty-third Canto of the Inferno.

But there were seventy-four pen and ink drawings, illustrating the Inferno, by Professor Scarramuzzo of Parma, which, in my opinion, were the gems of the whole exhibition. Fine photographs of these beautiful drawings were exhibited with them. My husband wrote for copies of them to Parma, as they could not be bought in Florence; they were sent, and are the most precious remembrances to me of the Dante festival.

There were also old portraits of several of Dante's contemporaries, or of persons mentioned in the Comedia. I noticed those of Guido Cavalcante and Christo Landini; most curious was an old wooden statue, covered with bronze, of Pope Boniface VIII., which was sent to the exhibition from the Archæological Museum of Bologna, with the following inscription:—

" Qui fui tratto ad onorar il trionfo
di lui ch'io cacciai dalla patria."*

One room was full of manuscripts on parchment, etc., of the Divina Comedia, some as old as the fourteenth century; and other books, especially Bibles, of the same date; and there were also some fragments of manuscripts by the Divine Poet himself, at which I looked with awe and reverence.

* " I was brought here to honour the triumph of him whom I sent into exile."

The exhibition contained also a large collection of arms, furniture, jewellery, and works of art of the middle ages, especially of the time of Dante; and which, examined in connexion with him, acquired a new interest.

The beautiful sword, the Gonfaloniere had presented to the King in the name of Florence, was also exhibited there. On one side of the blade were inscribed the words " Dante to the first King of Italy." On the other the following lines from the 6th Canto of the Purgatory:—

> " Vieni a veder la tua Roma, che piagne
> Vedova, sola, e dì e notte chiama:
> Cesare mio, perchè non m'accompagne?"

As at every festival there are many young ladies, who are not happy unless they get a dance, and as there are always gentlemen, who in order to enjoy themselves require races or regattas, and as the populace is every where fond of show and display, so there were also at the Dante festival balls, races, regattas, and tournaments. What those things could have to do with Dante, it would be difficult to say; for the love of God, of his country, and poetry, the three great elements of which the soul of the Divine Poet seems to have been composed, are not very intimately connected with these kinds of amusements. I think therefore they were out of keeping, and might as well have been omitted. A Dante festival, although rightly of a cheerful and joyful character, ought, it seems to me, always to be tempered by seriousness, and free from frivolity. I must however confess, that I went myself to look at these things whenever I was not too tired to do so.

The grand ball at the Casino, as the great clubhouse is called, in spite of the splendid ball-rooms, the good music and the elegant dress of the ladies, was rather a failure. The rooms were hot, and the ladies tired after the excitement of the day. Many seemed to prefer a walk through the open galleries, which were beautifully decorated with flowers, and where they could breathe the fresh night air, to a quadrille; and others withdrew to the many elegant rooms that join the two ball-rooms, preferring evidently a chat to a waltz. All retired at an early hour.

The popular ball, in the galleries of the Uffizi, was a much more novel and interesting thing.

The Uffizi, erected by Cosimo I., and considered Vasari's finest building, enclose a large court or square with porticos round it. One end is formed by a grand arch, under which stands the equestrian statue of Cosimo I., by Giovanni di Bologna, and all round, in niches in the wall, are placed well executed marble statues of great Tuscans by modern artists. There are about thirty in number, and among them such names as Leonardo da Vinci, Michael Angelo, Dante, Petrarca, Boccaccio, Lorenzo the Magnificent, Galileo, Benvenuto Cellini, etc. This vast and splendid place had been converted into an open air ball-room. It had been boarded all over. The walls and columns were covered with splendid Gobelin tapestry of grand designs and rich colouring. Large looking-glasses, encircled by garlands of flowers instead of frames, reflected and multiplied the innumerable lights, which poured their rays like fountains on the assembled multitude. In the middle of the square a fountain played among white, green, and red light, representing the Italian colours. Above, garlands of flowers and evergreens, from which thousands of coloured lamps were suspended, formed the plafond. Now and then the soft night breeze made the lamps swing gently backwards and forwards, which had a pretty effect. An excellent band played ball music. The centre was occupied by the dancers; the spectators moving along under the porticos, a quiet, polite, orderly crowd. I never heard a rude word nor was molested in the slightest degree during my walk round the porticos.

What surprised me however most was the extraordinary modesty and dignity of the Tuscan maidens, who had declined in a body to join the dance, considering the fête of too public a character. This seemed however not to interfere at all with the enjoyment of the ball. The young men thinking most probably that their sisters and sweethearts were right in what they did, danced among themselves, and evidently with no lack of spirit and enjoyment. They were mostly lads of between fifteen and twenty years of age. The young women, on the arm of their fathers, or in companies together, stood around as spectators and seemed to look on with pleasure. The festival concluded not unworthily with a series of " tableaux vivants " at the Teatro Pagliano, illustrating the life of Dante, and parts of the Divina Commedia. The former were accompanied by words set to music for the occasion; the latter preceded by those verses from the divine poem which they were intended to illustrate. The theatre is large, and every space was filled and prettily decorated with wreaths of flowers. Many of the tableaux were charming. The first meeting of Dante and Beatrice in the streets of Florence was lovely. The fiery graves of the Inferno, and the proud figure of Farinato, rising out of one, in order to speak to Dante, was the most effective. The one in which Pia in Purgatory speaks to the poet, will never be forgotten by me, because of the touching manner with which Mme. Ristori spoke the words :—

"Ricordati di me, che son la Pia,"

which sounded like an elegy.

Her recitation of the story of the unhappy Francesco da Rimini, was above all praise. Those sad words :—

" Nessun maggior dolore,
Che ricordarsi del tempo felice,
Nella miseria,"

moved me to tears. Splendidly did she pronounce her detestation of the licentious book that had wrought Francesca's fall, when she said :—

" Galeotto fu il libro e chi lo scrisse,"

and then added with a shudder of horror that trembled in her voice :—

" Quel giorno più non vi leggemmo avante."

Besides Madame Ristori, Sig. Salvini, Sig. Rossi, and Sig. Gottinelli, recited. They are considered the first actors in Italy, but I cannot say that they pleased me. Like those of Hamlet, " they imitated humanity so abominably." Their countrymen however applauded them the more, the more they " overstepped the modesty of nature;" "strutted and bellowed, and sawed the air with their hands." But the cheers which were so liberally bestowed upon these recitations, became most enthusiastic whenever the words could be interpreted so as to allude to the great political events and ideas of the day. At the words:—

> "Infin che 'l Veltro,
> Verrà, che la farà morir di doglia."
> *Infer. Canto* 1.

And at those,

> "Vieni a veder la tua Roma, che piagne,
> Vedova, sola, e dì e notte chiama :
> Cesare mio, perchè non m'accompagne?"
> *Purg. Canto* 6.

the audience forgot the "Divina Commedia" and the actors, and loudly cheered the King, who was present at the representation, and had been received with loud and continuous cheers when he entered his box.

But although the Dante festival is over, I cannot leave Florence without telling a little more about it, for the recollection of that charming town is one of the most pleasing of my journey.

Florence means, as everybody knows, the flowery, the blooming; but only those that have seen it in the month of May, can know how well it deserves so fair a name. The beautiful Tuscan valleys, in the most lovely of which Florence lies, may well be regarded as the garden of the temperate zone. It certainly seems to me the most perfect representation of it. Naples has a touch of the tropics; cacti, aloes, and palm trees, are not of our clime. We meet with nothing new or strange at Florence. We are quite at home, all among old friends, wearing a new and more beautiful dress than we were wont to see them in, and they please us more than ever.

The trees are not gigantic, but perfect in form and size. The meadows and fields, though a pleasant sight, are somewhat monotonous at home; here they have a perfectly different look. They are planted with rows of pretty young trees of all kinds, such as poplars, planes, may, mountain ashes, etc., which are not allowed to grow beyond the size of an ornamental garden tree, in order to prevent their giving too much shade. Round every stem twines a vine, that hangs gracefully from its supporting branches, and meets some other vine from a neighbouring tree, thus forming elegant festoons.

And how well the figures that animate this delightful landscape, harmonize with it. The women of Tuscany have not the stately beauty of the Roman matrons, nor the coquetish grace of their sisters of Milan and Venice. Their eyes have not the fire that burns in those of the Neapolitan girls, nor is their skin so fair as that of the Genoese; but I do not know if, after all, they are not the best looking in Italy. Their eyes have a soft lustre, which is very charming; their features are regular and very pleasing.

We stayed a few days after the festival under the false pretence of resting ourselves, but who could rest when there was so much to be seen and enjoyed?

I spent one day in the famous Gallery of the Uffizi, saw a splendid marble copy of Laocoon, and knew then what I never understood before, why that group is so much admired; saw the eternal ideal of Beauty, in the Venus of Medicis, and those wonderful beings which the brush of Titian has immortalised. But how can I venture to attempt enumerating all that I saw there? Another day was spent in the Palazzo Pitti, where some of Raphael's most charming works are treasured up. The " Madonna del Cardellino," the " Madonna del Baldacchino," which although very lovely, I hardly looked at, because I could not turn my eyes away from those two winged darlings that stand at her feet, and sing her praise; and there was above all my much beloved and revered " Madonna della Sedia."

I visited of course the churches, the interiors of which are mostly of a sombre grey, that blends with a lighter shade of the same colour, and with white. It produces a simple and serious effect. In striking contrast to the simple grandeur of the interior of these churches, is the Medicean chapel, belonging to the Church of St. Lorenzo, which is gorgeous in the extreme, the walls being entirely covered with costly marbles, and precious stones ; a fit monument of the overbearing pride and vanity of that famous family. It astonished me much, this monument of their untold wealth and great power ; I could not help contrasting with it the comparative simplicity and modesty of the Mausoleums of the great Sovereigns of our time, and felt that the most powerful and ambitious of them, could not build one for himself like the chapel of the Medici. In the sacristia of the same church, I saw the monuments on the tombs of Lorenzo and Giugliano dei Medici, by Michael Angelo. Of the six figures that compose the two monuments, the one of Lorenzo, made the deepest impression upon me. The whole figure, especially the face, has an expression of deep inconsolable grief. He looks as if sorrowing for ever that he robbed a great and noble people of its liberty ; as if come to a full knowledge of his guilt, and the sins and follies of his past life. I think some people say the expression of this sad, mournful figure sitting upon his own tomb, is one of meditation. Rogers writes " he scowls at us." It did not seem to me that he looks at any thing present at all, he looks with a vacant stare, his sight is turned inwardly, lost in the contemplation of the past.

I went directly from those tombs to the one where the great master reposes. It is in the church of Santa Croce, that the dust of Michael Angelo mingles with that of Galileo, and of many other great men. The allegorical figure of Italy sorrowing over the grave of Alfieri, who also rests within the walls of this church, is by Canova, and is as beautiful a monument as any poet could wish to have erected over his grave.

With a feeling not free from regret, we left Florence early one morning, in a fragrant May shower, that cooled and refreshed the air, and made the garden-country all around look fresher and lovelier than ever. We travelled in the same carriage with the well known Padre Gavazzi, who was not satisfied with the festival, as according to his opinion, it had not been of a character sufficiently decided political and religious.

When changing our carriage at Bologna, I

I suddenly found myself face to face with Mdlle. S—, and her father, who had been among our travelling companions from Trieste to Smyrna, and who were returning from their pilgrimage to Jerusalem. Their journey may have been one of intense enjoyment, it certainly had been one of great fatigue. The poor girl looked thin and worn, and spoke to me of her adventures with a woeful countenance. The expression of her face was at the same time exceedingly comical, and I could not help laughing at her tale, a laugh in which the good natured girl heartily joined, although it was partly at her own expense. According to her account, and her wan cheeks, and dim, lustreless eyes, confirmed what she said, the fatigues and dangers of the excursion to the Holy Land, must have been very great indeed. The Germans are not an equestrian nation. Of the forty excursionists, not one was a very proficient rider; in fact few of them had ever been on horse or donkey-back before. The consequence was an uninterrupted series of accidents as soon as travelling on horseback became, as it is everywhere in the East, the only mode of transit.

The poor girl had slipped off her horse with saddle and all, at a most dangerous spot in going to the Dead Sea; she might have been seriously injured, as she could not extricate herself at once, and the horse was moving on. Fortunately the young Kentuckian, who, as I had observed on the steamboat, was always trying to be near that "nice German girl," was close behind her. He jumped from his horse and caught hold of hers, so that she was able to get up, having sustained no great injury beyond the fright. She feelingly remarked, that fortunately her papa was far behind. He only heard of the accident, when the saddle and the young lady were safe again on the back of the steed. The poor man had been out of his saddle more than once, but without other injury than a sprain of his foot, which obliged him to lie down for a few days, and hurt him for many more.

Poor M. L—, a professor from Prague, did not escape so easily. In one of his falls he managed so badly that he hurt his leg seriously. Inflammation set in, and he had forty leeches applied to it. But what might have been the worst of all accidents, happened to Mme. de H—, the sister of the Archbishop. Horse and lady fell down together, and turned over and over before either got up again. The fair rider however escaped unhurt. I was sorry that there was no time for Mdlle. S. to tell me of all the accidents that befell these unlucky excursionists, for every one met with some mishap, either in Palestine or Egypt, with the exception of the four young Americans and old General T—. The latter seemed as much at home in Jerusalem and Cairo, as he had been on board the Neptune. He always ate with a tremendous appetite whatever the fare might be, and slept like a bear on whatever couch he rested.

The guard, who called out that the train for Milan was going to start, interrupted our conversation. Mdlle. S— took up a little box, which she had set down near her, and which contained a small tortoise, which poked its head through a hole in the lid. This and a shell, which she wore as a sign of her pilgrimage on her little hat, was, as far as I could see, all she had to recompense her for the endless troubles and fatigues of her journey.

And now I will hasten to conclude mine; for after we left Florence the journey no longer offered any great attractions. The places I saw now, I had already seen before, nor could they vie with those I had so lately visited. Now I was with heart and soul already in England, at home with my children. Oh, how slowly the express train travels! How long is a night in a railway carriage! Shall we rest a day at Paris? No, I am not tired.

I cross the Channel as in a dream. There are the white cliffs of Dover, I am in old England! Fly away train, rush along, take me home, home!

At last the train stops, a few minutes bring me to our garden gate. I fly through the garden, the door opens. Yes, there they are all, and all well! My baby climbs up a chair, and clings round my neck; the boys make a deafening noise, and I believe the mamma is almost as noisy.

And now I leave them, though for a few minutes only. I sit down in my own room, on my own chair, and all at once I feel I am tired. I shut my eyes, out of which tears steal, and my full heart thanks Him, who gave me the joys of the journey, who brought me safely home to my children and who watched over them, and preserved them while I was away.

THE END.

www.ingramcontent.com/pod-product-compliance
Lightning Source LLC
Chambersburg PA
CBHW020237170426
43202CB00008B/122